W9-CNH-951

PASSPORT
TAIWAN

Your Pocket Guide
to Taiwanese
Business,
Customs & Etiquette

Jeffrey E. Curry

Passport Series Editor: Barbara Szerlip

WORLD TRADE PRESS®
Professional Books for International Trade

World Trade Press
1505 Fifth Avenue
San Rafael, California 94901 USA
Tel: (415) 454-9934
Fax: (415) 453-7980
E-mail: WorldPress@aol.com

"Passport to the World" concept: Edward Hinkelman
Cover design: Peter Jones/Marge Wilhite
Illustrations: Tom Watson

This publication is designed to provide general information concerning the cultural aspects of doing business with people from a
particular country. It is sold with the understanding that the pub-
lisher is not engaged in rendering legal or any other professional
services. If legal advice or other expert assistance is required, the
services of a competent professional person should be sought.

LIbrary of Congress Cataloging-in-Publication Data

Curry, Jeffrey E. 1953 -
Passport Taiwan: your pocket guide to Taiwanese business, customs & etiquette / Jeffrey E. Curry
p. cm. -- (Passport to the world)
Includes bibliographical references.
ISBN 1-885073-27-5
1. Corporate culture -- Taiwan. 2. Business etiquette -- Taiwan. 3.
Industrial management -- Social aspects -- Taiwan. 4. Negotiation
in business -- Taiwan.
HD58. 7. C847 1997
390'. 0095124'9--dc21
97-8028
CIP

Printed in the United States of America

PASSPORT
TAIWAN

Passport To The World

Passport Argentina
Passport Brazil
Passport China
Passport France
Passport Germany
Passport Hong Kong
Passport India
Passport Indonesia
Passport Israel
Passport Italy
Passport Japan
Passport Korea
Passport Malaysia
Passport Mexico
Passport Philippines
Passport Russia
Passport Singapore
Passport South Africa
Passport Spain
Passport Thailand
Passport USA
Passport Vietnam

Table of Contents

Taiwan

The Watchful Tiger

Taiwan
Quick Look

Official name	Republic of China on Taiwan
Land area	35,751 sq km (13,803 sq mi)
Capital & largest city	Taipei
Elevations	
Highest	3,952 m (12,685 ft) (Mt. Yushan)
Lowest	sea level
People	
Population (1995)	21,500,000
Density	587 persons per sq km
Distribution	19% rural, 81% urban
Growth Rate	.93% per annum
Official language	Mandarin
Major religions	Buddhism, Taoism
Economy	
GDP (1995)	US$266 billion US$12,439 per capita
Principal trade partners	China, Hong Kong, Japan, U.S., ASEAN
Currency	New Taiwan Dollar (NT)
Exchange rate (1996)	NT$26 = US$1
Education and health	
Literacy(1995)	
Women	79%
Men	93%
Physicians	1 per 887 persons
Life expectancy	Women – 79 years Men –72 years
Infant mortality	5.6 per 1,000 live births

TAIWAN

Country Facts

Geography and Demographics

Located south of Japan and north of the Philippines in the western Pacific, Taiwan is comprised of a single large island and 80 smaller islets. Traditionally described as being shaped like a tobacco leaf, it covers roughly the same land area as the Netherlands or the combined U.S. states of Maryland and Delaware.

While some believe that Taiwan was originally part of mainland China, recent information shows that it arose separately from the sea roughly one million years ago. Its name derives from the southwestern port city of *Tainan*, which was called *Taivan* (terraced harbor) during the 17th century.

The main island has a fairly regular coastline, few natural ports, and mountain ranges that greatly limit the amount of usable land. Thus, the population of 21 million is concentrated on 25 percent of the available land — the second-highest population density in the world, just behind Bangladesh.

The Tropic of Cancer bisects the island, giving it a mixture of tropical and subtropical climates.

Temperatures range from a low of 16.6°C (62°F) in December to a high of 26.6°C (80°F) in July. Humidity averages 82 percent and rainfall often exceeds 2,500 millimeters (97.5 inches) annually. Typhoon season runs from July through early September.

Taiwan has few natural resources, with especially low deposits of petroleum, natural gas and coal. Although 60 percent of the island is timbered, strict environmental policies keep this resource untouchable. As a result, the island is a net importer of raw products, and this, in turn, has helped to make it a leader in value-added exports. Even with very limited arable land, it's become self-sufficient in rice and is a net exporter of pork, poultry and sugar. The island also produces 50 different types of fruit, is a recognized leader in the growing of high-grade teas, and maintains a sizable fishing fleet.

National Holidays

Founding Day . . . . January 1
  Celebrates founding of the Republic.
Youth Day . . . . March 29
  Children participate in special activities or outings.
Women's Day . . . . March 8
  Established in 1924, it celebrates motherhood.
Tomb Sweeping Day. . . . . . March 4 or 5
  Ancestors' graves are tended and offerings made. Corresponds with observance of Chiang Kai Shek's death.
Confucius's Birthday. . . . . . September 28
  Founder of Chinese culture honored with rites that include the waving of peacock feathers.
National Day (Double Ten) . October 10
  Commemorates fall of Qing Dynasty, which led to founding of Taiwan's Republic, with lavish parades.
Retrocession Day . . . . October 25
  Marks Taiwan's return to Chinese control from Japan after WWII.

Chiang Kai-shek's Birthday   October 31
> Reveres Kuomintang general who fought the Communists.

Sun Yat-sen's Birthday . . . . November 12
> Honors first president of the Republic, circa 1911.

Constitution Day . . . . December 25
> Celebrated somewhat like Christmas, it honors the island's constitutional rule.

Lunar New Year Festival . . . . January/February
> (See Chapter 16)

Dragon Boat Festival . . . . . mid-June
> A time for boat races and steamed rice dumplings (*zongzi*). Companies spend a lot of money sponsoring festival events.

Mid-Autumn Moon Festival. mid-September
> This harvest festival features firecrackers and the eating of rich "moon cakes."

Business Hours

Banks
Monday to Friday, 9 A.M. to 3:30 P.M.
Saturday 9 A.M. to noon
Offices
Monday to Friday, 9 A.M. to noon, 3:30 to 5:30 P.M.
Saturday, 9 A.M. to noon
Factories
Monday to Friday, 8 A.M. to noon, 1 to 5 P.M.
Government Offices
Monday to Friday, 8:30 A.M. to noon, 1:30 to 5:30 P.M.
Saturday, 8:30 A.M. to noon
Retail Stores
Monday to Friday, 9 A.M. to noon, 3:30 to 5:30 P.M.
Saturday and Sunday, 10 A.M. to 10 P.M.

Many urban convenience stores are open 24 hours a day. Similarly, restaurants of varying cuisines stay open almost around the clock.

2 The Taiwanese

First Inhabitants – First Explorers

Human habitation began on the island of Taiwan approximately 10,000 years ago, concentrated in the plains and along the coasts. Over time, the aboriginal tribes, mostly of Malay and Indonesian descent, would be pushed into the mountainous areas, but all maintain separate languages and cultures to this day. They constitute about 350,000 out of the island's more than 21-million-plus people.

During the Ch'in dynasty (221 – 06 B.C.), a Chinese commander named Hsu Fu was sent by the emperor to explore the eastern sea. Hsu Fu's encounter with an island he dubbed *I-chou* is seen as the first appearance of Taiwan on the Chinese horizon (although his description was sketchy). Chu Kuan, a later explorer sponsored by the Sui dynasty (A.D. 589 – 618), encountered an island he named *Liu Chiu*. At this same time, the Chinese navy journeyed to the Okinawa region, which they referred to as *Ryukyu*. Because confusion developed over these two island groups, Taiwan is still occasionally referred to in older texts as *Shao* (or Little) *Liu Chiu*.

The Hakka were the first of the Chinese to arrive in great numbers from the mainland. Starting in the 6th century, their migration was inspired by persecution in their home province of Henan. Although *Hakka* can be translated as "guest," it's unlikely that their arrival *en masse* on Taiwan was by invitation of the aboriginals. Today comprising 5 percent of the population, the Hakka remain a distinct social and linguistic group renowned for its disciplined work ethic.

Chinese from the Fukien coastal province began to arrive from across the Taiwan (a.k.a. Formosa) Strait in the early 15th century. They became the most populous group on the island, and the Taiwanese dialect is almost an exact duplicate of the Fukien dialect called *Amoy*. So close were the social and cultural ties that the mainland Chinese government came to view Taiwan as an extension of Fukien province long before formal annexation.

Traders & Invaders

Dutch traders arrived in the early 17th century and promptly named their anchorage *Ihla Formosa* (Island Beautiful). (The name *Formosa* would be used up until the mid-1970s, when it was replaced by *Taiwan*, in order to lend legitimacy to the island as a Chinese seat of government.) In 1624, the Dutch decided to mount a fullscale invasion and set up headquarters in the southwestern city of Tainan. The Spanish arrived in northern Taiwan two years later and remained until the Dutch expelled them in 1641. Then, in 1661, the Dutch themselves were expelled — by arriving Ming dynasty armies led by Cheng Ch'en-kung, whose 30,000 troops were looking for respite from the onslaught of the Manchus on the mainland. Fearing an immediate return of Cheng Ch'en-kung and hoping to deny him a sympathetic population, the Manchus attempted to move Fuk-ien's coastal occupants inland at least 30 *li* (10 miles). This backfired, causing the first sizable migration from Fukien to Taiwan as the forcibly displaced fish-ermen and farmers sought a new life. During this same period, Spain began to have suspicions that Cheng Ch'en-kung had designs on the Philippines. Taking more drastic population control measures than the Manchus, Spain's government had its army slaughter 10,000 Manila-based Chinese. Infuriated, the newly installed Taiwanese military ruler began plans for invading the Philippines. However, he died suddenly and was replaced by his son Cheng Ching, who neglected to follow through with his father's retaliation scheme.

After Ching's death (and 20 years of watchful waiting), the Manchus decided to take advantage of the ensuing succession squabbles. In 1683, they sent General Shih Lang to Taiwan with orders to establish dominion over the Ming bastion. The Ming armies were defeated and General Shih went on to seize the whole island within the year. It was given *fu* status, which classified it as a frontier territory. For the next two centuries, mainland immigrants (mostly Fuk-ienese) poured onto the island, which was now under the direct control of Fukien province.

Japanese Tenure

In 1884, France attempted to expand its territo-rial claims in Southeast Asia by staging an invasion of the Taiwan island group. They were repulsed, and in 1886, Taiwan was designated as a separate prov-ince in order to bolster Chinese claims of sover-eignty. It was at this time that the capital of the island was moved from Tainan to Taipei under its new gov-ernor, Liu Ming-chu'an. Lu built the island's first electrical power plant and railroad, extended educa-

tion to all island inhabitants (at the time, more than
2.5 million), and insisted that Western science be
taught alongside Chinese philosophy.

In 1895, conflicts over territorial rights on the
Korean Peninsula resulted in the Sino-Japanese War.
China was handily defeated and had to cede its
interests in Korea, with Taiwan being handed over
as an additional prize — a loss that particularly dis-
mayed the Chinese. More than 1,200 *chu-jen* (schol-
ars equivalent to Ph.Ds) protested the move. China
even asked that Britain or France be allowed to over-
see the island, rather than have it fall into the hands
of the Japanese. All requests were denied.

Unwilling to accept their new Japanese rulers,
Taiwanese residents revolted for a brief but spirited
period. The Japanese crushed the rebellion and
ruled, often quite harshly, until the end of World
War II. The infamous Decree No. 21 declared that
Taiwanese citizens could be arrested and confined
without trial for such petty violations as "being
rude" or "fabricating rumors." What education the
Taiwanese were permitted to receive was strictly
technical in nature and decidedly inferior to what
Japanese students received. Much of the island's
early industrial base was installed by the Japanese
government and was used to advance their now
openly expansionist goals.

In spite of such harsh inequities, the Japanese
influence still abounds on the island; it's sometimes
cited as a main contributor to Taiwan's success in
the postwar period. Much of the educational and
industrial infrastructure installed by Japan still
remains, as well as a large number of Japanese
speakers. Accordingly, Taiwan continues to be a frequent travel spot for Japanese tourists. However,
Japan's economic effect on Taiwan is a continued
source of controversy.

Seeds of Division

As far back as 1911, internal political trouble had been rising as China tried to rid itself of dynastic governments. After the fall of the Ching dynasty, Sun Yat-sen's rule of the new *Republic of China* was short-lived, and in 1916, a period of open civil war erupted as the result of an attempt to restore the emperorship by Yuan Shihkai. A semblance of unity was restored by Chiang Kai-shek and his Kuonmintang (KMT or Nationalist) Party, though they were continually dogged by communist rebels and Japanese pre–World War II military posturing.

In 1931, under the guise of creating an "Asia for Asians," the Japanese seized Manchuria as an extension of their plans for a Greater Prosperity Zone. In 1937, the Japanese army invaded the rest of China, including Taiwan, seeking further access to natural resources and manpower. During World War II, much bloody fighting and reports of civilian massacres occurred on the mainland. Both the Communists and the Kuonmintang forces battled the invaders to eventual victory, only to resume their civil war after 1945. As part of the Potsdam Proclamation of that same year, China was granted the return of Taiwan as a reward for assisting the Allies against Japan. Taiwan's economy had been depleted by the Japanese war effort, with much of its resources evacuated to Japan and its manpower lost to forced labor. For a few years the islanders tried to regroup, but they were once again over-whelmed by events on the mainland of China.

Two Governments, One Island

By 1949, facing defeat in its civil war with the Communists, the KMT made a tactical withdrawal to Taiwan. This added 900,000 civilians and 600,000 troops to the island's population of 6 million. An invasion by communist troops was averted by their preoccupation with events in Korea and by the presence in the Taiwan Strait of the KMT's military ally, the United States.

Believing themselves to be the rightful rulers of all China, the KMT viewed their new headquarters in Taipei as a temporary billet. The KMT set about rebuilding Taiwan's dilapidated economy while brooking no political opposition from the islanders. Heavy emphasis on industrialization, copious American support, and sweeping land reform made Taiwan one of the new "Asian Tigers" by the 1960s. Meanwhile, these same three facets were revamping Japan and South Korea.

This postwar period saw the division of the island's population into two main groups. While a wide variety of groups coexist, all citizens whose families arrived in Taiwan before the end of World War II are referred to as *Taiwanese*. They comprise roughly 70 percent of the population. Chinese with Taiwanese citizenship who arrived after that date are thought of as *mainlanders*, though intermarriage is so common that it blurs the distinction.

China Rattles Its Saber

Taiwan was internationally recognized as the Republic of China until 1971, when growing pressure from "Red" China forced the United Nations to oust the island, thus favoring the mainland as the "official" China. Even the U.S., Taiwan's most ardent supporter, switched its diplomatic recognition in 1979 — just four years after the death of Chiang Kai-shek.

Relegated to the status of "renegade province," its diplomats relieved of their negotiating portfolios, Taiwan concentrated on economic growth.

International political affiliations with the U.S. and its allies remained strong, albeit unofficial, and China made few loud noises about Taiwan's status for the next ten years.

The KMT continued to rule Taiwan (as its sole political party) with Chiang Kai-shek's son, Ching-kuo, at the helm. Martial law had been in effect since 1949. Then, in 1986, the Democratic Progressive Party made a successful bid for recognition and gained seats in the legislature. Chiang Ching-kuo declared the end of martial law in 1987, shortly before his death. The year 1989 saw the first true election in Taiwan (with the KMT still maintaining a 70 percent majority of seats) and the island's first native Taiwanese president, Lee Teng-hui.

During the 1980s, the British government had negotiated the 1997 return of Hong Kong to China, with an agreement to start phasing in Chinese influence as of 1989. The Chinese government saw this as an opportunity to start a campaign to have their "historical" rights to Taiwan recognized as well. However, Taiwan's 1989 economy vastly exceeded the mainland's, especially on a per-capita basis. This made China's sovereignty claim appear ludicrous and more of a grasp at a readymade capitalist economy than any long-standing right. China was attracting investments of its own and saw how political turmoil had adversely affected its economy after the 1989 student killings in Tiananmen Square. Hoping to cause a similar (but longer-term) effect, China started threatening to invade.

After Hong Kong, Taiwan?

Foreign investment in Taiwan duly tapered off, and the Taiwanese themselves began to move some of their assets off the island. Oddly enough, mainland China and Vietnam (both reforming communist economies and mutual, ancient enemies) were major recipients of this now-declining investment. Taiwan was demonstrating its longtime mastery of hedging its bets. President Lee entered the fray by publicly taunting the Chinese, calling their bluff on regular occasions. Even Lee's attendance at his college reunion in the U.S. was treated by the Chinese as a major political slap in the face; China sought to have his visa status denied by Washington, D.C. In 1996, China went so far as to commence what it called "rocket testing" off the shores of Taiwan, just prior to Taiwanese national elections. The international condemnation that followed left China unsure of how to influence world opinion in its favor against Taipei.

Lee triumphed in reelection, erasing any hope China may have had that the Taiwanese could be intimidated further. Diplomatic and international investment reaction made it clear that the world will be paying close attention to the consequences of Hong Kong's return to the "motherland." In the meantime, the mainland remains committed to preventing Taiwanese independence.

Language

Hakka, Japanese and aboriginal languages are spoken in addition to the main language, Taiwanese (which is similar to the mainland Fukien dialect, *Amoy*). English is fast becoming the second language of Taiwan, primarily because of its predominance in international commerce. Fluency in English, the American dialect in particular, is considered an indicator of both education and urbanity.

Mandarin Chinese (called *Kuo-yu* or "national language" on Taiwan and *Putonghua* or "common tongue" on the mainland) is the language of government, TV and radio. Spoken, it's very similar to mainland Mandarin, but in its written form, the Taiwanese use more traditional Chinese characters (which is one of the reasons why they believe themselves to be the true keepers of Chinese culture). They also pride themselves on grammatical and calligraphic excellence.

Mandarin and its dialects (Shanghai, Hakka, Fukien and Cantonese) are tonal and require a vast amount of vocabulary for mastery. Whole words can be represented by single characters, and fluency demands the knowledge of more than 6,000 symbols. As is true of many Asian languages, pronunciation must be precise in order to achieve the correct meaning. Westerners often have difficulty achieving the proper tones, as some of these require a different use of facial and lingual muscles than English or other Romance languages do. Conversely, Mandarin speakers have difficulty with European languages. English words of Chinese origin include: *tea, typhoon, sampan, kumquat, kowtow* and *shanghai.*

Ancient Philosophy – High-Tech Lives

Taiwan is traditionally Buddhist, with strong Taoist and Confucian influences. Like the Japanese, they've managed to reconcile these ancient belief systems with lives steeped in 20th-century technology. They follow the Eightfold Path of Buddha (right view, right thought, right speech, right behavior, right livelihood, right effort, right mindfulness, right concentration) as well as the related Taoist principles of freedom from desire and a quest for simplicity.

These principles fit into the hierarchical social structure demanded by Confucius more than 2500 years ago. The ruler dominates the people, the husband the wife, the parent the child, the older the younger. Subordinates display fidelity in return for wise and munificent decisions from above. Because it is basically a seniority system, each player hopes to one day rise to the top by virtue of age.

Buddhism, Taoism and Confucianism are practiced as philosophies rather than as religions, for the most part, and a wide variety of gods can be accommodated under this philosophical aegis. Lao Tzu (the founder of Taoism) and Confucius (K'ung Tzu) were contemporaries and much of their philosophy overlaps. However, whereas Lao Tzu believed "nothingness" to be ultimate state of being, Confucius believed in the centrality of relationships, that respect, duty, loyalty, sincerity, humility and courage should shape every aspect of existence.

Christianity, Catholicism and Islam have followers here. *I-kuan Tao* (Religion of One Unity) brings together the tenets of most of the world's faiths and is practiced widely. Indigenous religions include *Chai Chiao, Hsia Chiao, Li-Chiao* and *T'ien Te Chiao*.

"Face" & Ren Ching Wei

In the Confucian system, the maintaining of "face" (*mien-tzu*) is of paramount importance. Westerners tend to view life as a series of ups and downs, tempered with the hope of a successful outcome: two steps forward, one step back. But within Taiwan's hierarchical society, any step backward is considered almost permanent and a major violation of the relationship code. If a person causes his or her own "loss of face," then they've misused the loyalty and respect of their subordinates. If the subordinates cause the loss, then they've violated the social contract by not showing respect and thus "lose face" as well. If someone from outside of the relationship causes a loss of face, then the outsider has insulted the whole group. Any praise will be denied repeatedly, and excessive praise may be considered insulting — since it attempts to raise someone above their natural *mien-tzu.*

Another important key to Taiwanese society is *ren ching wei* (literally, the flavor of human emotion). It means being sincere and considerate, and therefore civilized. For example, modesty dictates that a Taiwanese turn down a gift when it's first offered. A giver shows *ren ching wei* by continuing to offer it two or three times. If the giver is a foreigner, his gesture also exhibits *ren ching wei* by showing that he respects the Taiwanese way of doing things.

Seeking Knowledge Abroad

The Taiwanese recognize the complexity and diversity of nations beyond their own borders. They are, in fact, some of the most traveled people in Asia. Rarely will visitors encounter an intense *gwielo* or "foreign devil" reaction (common in mainland China) from a people who've been designated foreigners in their own land.

The Taiwanese recognize much of their success has come from the technological and financial input of advanced Western cultures and, to a some degree, from Japan. The island sends thousands of students overseas every year to obtain the best education possible, with the vast majority in the U. S.

Because of their geographic isolation, the Taiwanese fan outward to find cultural, financial and technical resources with which to advance their fellow citizens. This mission sometimes comes at great personal cost, as it may require separation from family members and the all important *group.* Sacrifice for the sake of group is not unique to the Taiwanese, but their sense of mission is seldom matched elsewhere.

The Taiwanese Individual

The Taiwanese see themselves as "special Chinese," because they've preserved the *original* China during the last five decades of communist rule and cultural purges. They take this preservationist role very seriously and actively promote their cultural primacy. This is exemplified by the recent touring art exhibit *Treasures of Imperial China,* which was actually comprised of artifacts from Taipei museums.

The subordination of the individual to the group has resulted in group decision making, a process that Westerners find slow and inefficient. However, their worldliness has increased their sense of individuality and thus their ability to act alone.

Attitudes Toward Foreigners

Terms for non-Taiwanese, particularly Westerners, range from *lau wai* (old foreigner) to *yang gwei* (foreign devil) to *da bi dz* (big nose) to *ang mo* (red beard). Hairiness is thought to indicate a lower level of evolution, as is dark skin (Taiwanese farm women traditionally cover themselves from head to toe when working outdoors, in the hottest, most humid seasons). And being left-handed is seen as odd, though the left hand isn't considered unclean, as in other parts of Asia.

Westerners are also often seen as lacking patience, making an insincere show of friendship, being selfish and intolerant of other cultures, being "soft" from having grown up in comfort, and underestimating the value of teamwork.

3   Cultural Stereotypes

Overly Respectful of Authority

The Taiwanese do what they're told, blindly and without question.

Confucian philosophy dictates people in high positions be given respect. This dates from a time when few had the privilege of an education and the possibility of achieving power. Age is also respected, harkening back to a time when surviving to old age was a major accomplishment. Even today, sons are dismissed from family-run businesses and disgraced for not exhibiting the proper amount of piety.

The Taiwanese tread a narrow path between the Confucian hierarchy and the "information highway" hierarchy of the late-20th century. Many elders recognize their own lack of "modern" information and privately defer to their subordinates. However, public face is always maintained.

Unable to Show Emotion

Taiwanese are cold and only open up to family.

Emotional outbursts of any kind, whether friendly or unfriendly, are considered to be a loss of control and therefore lacking in Buddhist merit. As in most Buddhist-based cultures, people here prefer to reserve their warmth and hospitalities for those they know well.

It's also true that the Taiwanese live in one of the most densely populated areas on the planet (587 people per square kilometer). Privacy is a rarity. The inhabitants of main cities like Taipei have succumbed to the "disease" of emotional detachment, brought on by the harshness of urban life. Taiwan is, after all, a thriving technological economy. Visitors may find it somewhat cheerless at first glance.

Western Wannabees

The Taiwanese are poor imitators of the great technological powers.

Many Westerners (especially Americans) complain that Asia (Taiwan in particular) should just quit fighting progress and adopt the Western way of doing things. After all, the argument goes, Asia hasn't invented anything in several thousand years; all they do is tinker with Western technology and economic systems. (The supremacy of the group in Taiwanese culture is cited as a chief cause.) Why not just accept the best-that-money-can-buy package?

Westerners (and even some Asians, like the Japanese) must understand that for anyone of a Chinese-derived culture, "modern life" isn't necessarily the best of all possible options. Nations like the U.S., with a heritage of only a couple of centuries, have yet to stand the test of time. The Taiwanese wish to adapt to modernity gradually and in their own way, though to a much greater degree than the mainland Chinese do. As one local adage puts it: *The stomach must wait for the mouth.*

Cultural Snobs

The Taiwanese think that they're vastly superior.

The Taiwanese see themselves as the culmination of a culture that dates back several millennia. It would be hard for anyone with this lineage not to see themselves as being a cut above.

The Taiwanese know that Westerners aren't particularly impressed with ancient history ("So what have you done lately?") and that the Japanese see Chinese culture as a hodgepodge, at best. The Taiwanese are only trying to combat the foreigner's own cultural snobbery when they display the depths of Taiwanese-Sino culture. Another adage: *Fish can be caught in a deep pool as well as in a shallow one.*

Mini-China

Taiwan is just a pretend-China that will eventually be reabsorbed.

On the surface, Taiwan is Chinese in both language and custom. (The same could have been said about the U.S. and Great Britain in the early-19th century.) Taiwan does respect its Chinese roots but there's great divergence of thought on the island as to whether there's but *one* China.

Elder members of the ruling Kuomintang would like to see one China, with their party at the helm. Other Taiwanese see a future dominated by the mainland and with diminished support from Western powers. Younger islanders envision a separate Taiwan in which freedom and economic growth will maintain their lifestyles. This new generation has no desire to live under a communist political system in which "socialist free market" economics deliver wages that are a mere 5 percent of Taiwan's levels.

Regional Differences

The Taiwanese culture is homogeneous, for the most part. Any distinctions are based on urban and pastoral roots, rather than on ethnic divisions. True to the nature of insular nations, ethnicity and regionalism are put aside to create a seamless front against common enemies: in this case, mainland China. Even the aboriginal groups (once considered the objects of derision) are viewed as a useful source for acquiring hard currency from tourism.

North, South, East & West

Development has taken place primarily in the north, the southwest, and along the central west coast. Even a casual glance at a good map reveals the population concentrations.

Taipei, the national focal point of both politics and finance, receives the bulk of the congestion and pollution. The remainder of the northern part of the island, though sprinkled with some beautiful scenery, plays off of its proximity to the capital. Northern Taiwan, home to the KMT, is where all of the country's growth in the 20th century was planned and initiated.

The central west coast is a popular resort and tourism area with stunning mountain views. Its coastal areas are prime rice producers and many of its towns sponsor elaborate religious festivals.

The southwest, another highly industrialized area, is home to Kaohsiung, a major seaport and the world's fourth-largest container port. Another feature of the southwest is the municipality of Tainan. The former capital of Taiwan, it continues to be the center for Taiwanese culture, and its 200 temples make it a center for Buddhist and Confucian worshippers.

The east coast of Taiwan is dominated by the two counties of Hualien and Taitung. The lack of industrial development here is the result of mountainous terrain and frequent typhoons. Occasional earthquakes haven't helped matters. Many of the country's larger aboriginal tribes, such as the Ami, live here, and they're partly responsible for the area's growing tourist trade. It's also fast becoming the site of expensive vacation homes. Many areas remain inaccessible by road; it wasn't until 1980 that a railroad line was finally completed here.

The major island group, P'eng-hu, is devoted to fishing. (The Portuguese called them the *Pescadores* or Fishermen Islands.) This small archipelago was the point of entry of most of the Portuguese, Dutch, French and Japanese invasions. Because of the continued threat, Taiwan maintains numerous military installations on these islands as well as on others located in the strait between P'eng-hu and the mainland. The islands off the east coast — Lanyu (Orchid) and Lutao (Green) — are primarily tourist attractions. Liuchiu, off the southern coast, is gradually making the transition from aquaculture to tourism.

5

Government & Business

The Past Meets the Future

Taiwan is one of the five "Tigers of Asia," a distinguished group that includes Japan, South Korea, Singapore and Hong Kong. Like its comembers, Taiwan has seen the virtues of a close relationship between government and business (with government in charge) and used its easy access to foreign markets and ability to protect domestic commerce to build a strong economy within what could be called a "controlled free market."

Released from Japanese control after World War II, Taiwan was faced with a depleted economy. The Chinese government was in no position to help. When Chiang Kai-shek arrived in 1949 with the KMT to declare Taiwan *the* Republic of China, his first agenda, after entrenchment, was economic renewal. The 1950s was a time of major land reform, which revitalized the agricultural sector. At the same time, a policy of import substitution helped revive manufacturing while protecting foreign currency reserves. These same policies are being implemented in Eastern Europe today.

Taiwan Rising

In the 1960s, the government turned from import substitution to direct foreign investment encouraged with tax incentives. This change came at the end of major U.S. redevelopment aid in 1965. Growth was now seen in terms of expanded exports and the exploitation of the island's educated (but poorly paid) labor. "Made in Taiwan" took over from "Made in Japan" as the catchphrase for cheap production and dubious quality.

In the 1970s, the Taipei government moved to the next phase of development: industrial infrastructure. Capital-intensive heavy industries such as steel and petrochemicals were emphasized and aided. As part of the Ten Major Construction Projects Directive, highways and air transportation were improved. Also during this period, many of Taiwan's students were sent abroad to secure the technical training needed to advance the country's place in global economics.

In the 1980s, recognizing its geographic and demographic limitations, Taiwan moved into the higher value-added technical industries. Establishment of the Hsinschu Science Park just outside of Taipei (Taiwan's "Silicon Valley"), along with incentives for joint ventures by Western (particularly U.S.) companies helped push the island to the high-tech forefront.

The Six-Year National Development Plan announced in 1992 called for 775 projects demanding more than US$300 billion, in areas ranging from new highways to state-of-the-art research and development facilities, to nuclear power plants — all overseen by the government. In Taiwan, government isn't seen as an impediment to business but as its incubator.

In mid-1997, the Ministry of the Interior opened Taiwan's property market to foreign investment for the first time. Investors are required to set up corporations and to promote six general principles, including environmental protection and "promotion of the quality of life."

One of the government's most ambitious projects is to turn the country into a major transportation hub for international commerce in the southwestern Pacific. For this to happen, it's counting on the decline of Hong Kong and the stillbirth of Shanghai as free trade centers.

Exports, Imports & Diminishing Red Tape

Taiwan has skillfully manipulated its export and import laws to its advantage, blatantly discriminating against foreigners in the process. Although the government has long supported the advancement of exports as hard currency earners, its paperwork and regulatory atmosphere are complex. Foreign firms operating in Taiwan are often amazed by the amount of red tape they encounter. Keep in mind that Confucian bureaucracies emphasize form (or in this case, forms) over function. Although nowhere near as extreme as the bottlenecks found in China or Vietnam, governmental processes here can be time-consuming. Patience is required.

Since the late 1980s, the government has taken steps to reduce its paperwork; it claims that 70 percent of the products available for export now require no licensing. It established Export Processing Zones (EPZs) in Kaohsiung and Taichung, within which manufacturers can locate factories whose products can be exported duty free. The Science-Based Industrial Park at Hsinchu offers duty-free exporting for high-tech manufacturers while discouraging domestic sales with high import duties.

Import laws started to loosen up in the early 1990s as a result of Taiwan's continued need to keep its trading partners (especially the U.S. and Japan) happy. Up until that point, Taiwan had only encouraged the importation of needed raw materials. Taiwan continues to have generous "re-export" policies for raw materials brought in for eventual manufacture into finished products. However, in its continued attempt to be a "global player," Taiwan now imports many finished goods. In fact, it's one of the top 20 importers in the world.

The Tiger Meets the Dragon

Still, Taiwan's future is hardly secure. China is intent on returning the island to its fold. Troop buildups and war games in Fukien province across the Taiwan Straits aren't merely for show, and the government of Lee Teng-hui knows it. As Taiwan's military allies desert it, Taipei is playing a waiting game. It hopes to bring in sufficient foreign investment to make an attack unsavory, while at the same time moving some of its own assets offshore (even to China), in case the worst happens.

It's also counting on the fact that any aggressive move by China would greatly upset Japan and South Korea — both of whom harbor long-standing feuds with Beijing. And that would likely bring the U.S. into the conflict. Taiwan's greatest hope is that China will realize that in today's increasingly "globalized" world, wars are bad for business.

Crisis of Confidence

In 1996, a county magistrate was murdered in his home along with seven others. The next month, a Taiwanese mayor was investigated for allegedly taking NT$4 million (US$143,600) in bribes, a magistrate got a life sentence for corruption charges, the director of women's affairs for the opposition Democratic Progressive Party was murdered by a taxi driver, and a township chairman was charged with kidnapping seven councillors and threatening to "cut their legs off" if they didn't vote for him. One figure puts the year's crime rate jump at 18 percent.

Then in May, 1997, something unprecedented happened. After the daughter of a local TV entertainer was abducted on her way to school, then tortured and killed — an "ordinary" citizen this time, a teenage girl — some 50,000 middle-class citizens took to the streets demanding that President Lee apologize for his "mistakes" (he had stated publicly that national development was more important than a schoolgirl's murder), that Lee's cabinet be replaced, and that Prime Minister Lien Chan resign. Two weeks later, 100,000 took to the streets. Several cabinet officials subsequently quit, including the KMT's most popular public figure, Ma Ying-jeou (who said that he was "disappointed" by his colleagues reluctance to take responsibility for Taiwan's problems.)

Much of the public discontent stems from the widely held belief that the government is focused on foreign affairs, with little or no interest in domestic reform. And many blame Taiwan's rapid democratization, which replaced 1980s martial law with a 1990s "fast-money mentality" and a cultural rootlessness. Others are concerned that the government might opt for a relatively simple solution to the public's fury by reinstating the old system. And still others wonder if the current backlash will lose momentum or dissipate before it can bring about the hard work of social and civic change.

6   The Work Environment

The Dynamics of Confucian Management

Taiwan's labor force is consistently ranked in the top ten worldwide. Both white collar and blue collar workers exhibit a high degree of training and education. Management styles generally fall between the autocratic and bureaucratic with smatterings of entrepreneurial laissez-faire. Still, all management is Confucian at base, which means that employees are expected to provide unquestioning obedience (not innovation) in return for wise and paternal leadership.

In the last decade, a great deal of emphasis has been put on such technical fields such as engineering and computer sciences — the result of incoming foreign investment and the nation's emphasis on exports. Shipping and manufacturing have also dominated the labor market. Retailing, marketing and investment services have only recently received attention. As Taiwan's wages began to grow, exceeding its competition in developing Asia (Taiwan's labor is currently 20 times as expensive as China's!) manufacturing started to move offshore.

Like that of its nearby rival Japan, Taiwan's work ethic was born of hardship and the need to catch up. The post–World War II years were an era of self- sacrifice, and no task was thought too difficult if it advanced the nation. But younger Taiwanese have only known a successful Taiwan and, like younger Japanese, they've begun to imitate the consumer and work habits of their Western counterparts.

Many businesses observe *shou shei*, a midday rest period for employees. The average vacation is two weeks (ten working days), plus eight paid days are allotted for attending weddings, three to eight days are allotted for funerals, and those on sick leave receive half pay for up to 30 days. The minimum wage is US$572 per month.

Feng Shui & Dragon Dances

The Taiwanese believe that fortune can be influenced by the positioning of physical objects. Before a building is constructed or remodeled, a *feng shui* (wind and water) practitioner is summoned. The placement of doors and windows, the arrangement of furniture and the nearness to bodies of water are considered on the basis of their ability to attract good forces and repel evil ones.

The *feng shui* man may recommend the remedial placement of mirrors and chimes. *Feng Shui* is taken seriously by everyone from rural villagers to corporate executives; even Western companies operating here hire *feng shui* practitioners in order to keep local employees comfortable.

The Dragon Dance features a long line of dancers who perform a serpentine march, covered by a silken "skin." Because dragons are credited with the power to expel evil forces, the dance is often performed at the opening of new businesses — accompanied by much drumming and cymbal crashing.

Women in Business

Taiwanese women have had the vote since the republic was founded (all voters must be at least 20), but in terms of child custody, men were the sole legal "owners" of their offspring until 1994.

In the workplace, laws regarding mandatory overtime and graveyard shift assignments greatly favor women. Also, women can't be required to work between the hours of 10 P.M. and 6 A.M. without government approval. An eight-week maternity leave at full wages is guaranteed for those who've been employed at least six months. The downside of women's "special" status is that they earn about US$475 less per month than their male counterparts, and when it comes to social or career advancement, they're at a distinct disadvantage (though the Taiwanese are currently far more progressive in their treatment of women than the mainland Chinese).

Because of its cosmopolitan atmosphere and high level of economic sophistication, Taiwan has (for Asia at least) a large number of women heading companies — usually in the service and retail sectors, rather than in manufacturing or high tech. The head of Taiwan's automobile company, Yue-loong Motors, is one exception to this rule. Other notable Taiwanese women include Dr. Shirley W. Y. Kuo (the first female cabinet minister, a former Minister of Finance, and a professor of economics at National Taiwan University) and Hsiao Chuang Kuo (a famous dance artist).

On the Homefront

Much of Sino-Asia culture maintains a clear demarcation between womens' public and private roles. However, the acquiescing female and the domineering male exchange roles almost immediately upon crossing the family threshold. Men here may be the breadwinners, but they don't control their home environments. Wives, mothers and mothers-in-law generally call the shots and make the major decisions regarding children.

Because it ceased to be an agricultural economy some decades ago, Taiwan has little need of large families to till its fields. This has allowed women to pursue careers beyond motherhood. However, there's no one-child-per-couple mandate, as in mainland China. Birth control use has increased from 24 percent in 1965 to 81 percent in 1996, with the average family decreasing from six children to three.

Education opportunities for women are widely available to middle-class families for both domestic and overseas study. Taiwanese men tend to marry women whose educational status is similar to their own. Families are willing to support a daughter's pursuit of higher education in the belief that it will either enlarge the number of her marriage prospects or increase the family's overall earning capacity should she remain single. Similar family-based motivators are applied to advancing a son's education.

An unmarried son is just as big of an embarrassment and a source of pity to a Sino-Asian family as an unmarried daughter. (Many divorced people remarry to avoid this stigma.) However, men can marry at any age, while women are considered permanent "old maids" after the age of 30. Married career women who decide against having children will be perceived of as "barren" and may be pressured into adopting a child or two from the mainland.

Strategies for Foreign Businesswomen

Female business travelers here aren't uncommon, but the Taiwanese (male and female alike) may be quite surprised to find a woman as the lead player in a business or governmental delegation. Foreign companies must make an extra effort to ensure that their female executives will be treated properly. Consider the following:

- Prior to arrival, all correspondence should come from the female executive's office, with her job title prominently in evidence.

- Because foreign names are as confusing to the Taiwanese as their names are to non-Taiwanese (and often difficult to distinguish by gender), make a point of noting the executive as *Miss* or *Mrs.*

- When forwarding a list of the members of the delegation, take care to place the female executive name and job title at the top and, if possible, print it in a larger or bold font for emphasis.

- When arriving at meetings, have a subordinate manager introduce the executive last while making a very specific reference to her status as the leader of the delegation.

- When printing up business cards (see Chapter 15), the executive's job title should be translated to the highest corresponding Taiwanese title possible.

- Make sure all important points are directed to the executive and that all subordinates act very deferentially to her input.
- Under no circumstances should any member of the delegation argue with or contradict the executive during the meeting.

Many foreign businesswomen make a point of not calling attention to their gender when dealing with staff in their home country. You may find it awkward to brief your subordinates on the topics stated above without seeming too heavy-handed. You must keep in mind that, for female executives, meetings in Taiwan are going to be uphill battles. There's no sense starting at the bottom of the hill.

When the Female Exec is Number Two

Male team leaders working with a female second-in-command should make sure that their Taiwanese counterparts understand the seriousness and responsibilities of her position and that they don't mistake her for a secretary, or worse, a mistress. All innuendo should be dealt with sternly and professionally. "Laughing it off" won't help in the long run and will, in fact, serve to render your "right hand" useless.

Female executives here assume, rightly or wrongly, that Westerners are far less apprehensive about doing business with a woman than Taiwanese males are. Taiwanese businesswomen already feel that they have a lot to prove to their staffs, so you'll best serve your own interests by treating them as equals. Do your homework. Find out whom you'll be meeting with (including gender) and treat them accordingly. A good translator will go a long way toward assisting you in this area.

8 Making Connections

The Guanxi System

Taiwan has considerable commercial holdings around the world. It has operated with equal success in both complex business environments and in emerging markets, adopting and adapting to virtually every economy in the world. Because of this, they're well-schooled in the *modus operandi* of foreign companies. When you arrive in Taiwan, they'll already be familiar with your business style, though you may not know their's.

If you wish to operate on their turf you must come to recognize the value of the *relationship*. Before contracts are even discussed, let alone signed, the Taiwanese will be sizing up you and your company's other representatives as *people*, not just as potential associates. Because Taiwanese commercial law is quite limited by Western standards, most domestic business is conducted among friends, friends of friends, and family. This system of *guanxi* (connections) has served Sino-Asia for centuries.

An important aspect of the all-important relationship is how much face you and your company have in the marketplace. If you have an internationally recognized brand name that will lend prestige to your Taiwanese partner, a relationship will be easily established. Smaller companies will have to make a greater effort to demonstrate their value, or potential value.

It warrants mentioning that the system of *guanxi* in Taiwan is not as stringent as it is in mainland China. The Taiwanese enjoy much greater flexibility and have a healthy respect for entrepreneurs. And unlike many emerging Asian economies, they don't fear fast-moving projects. The "relationship" is considered more of a courtesy then a necessity and is most conspicuous in its absence than its presence. Failure to build significant *guanxi* will not destroy a project in Taiwan but it will certainly slow progress.

When in Rome. . . .

Courtesy is central to Sino-Asian culture. Foreign businesspeople must observe social niceties if a project is to move along. The Taiwanese have made a habit of adapting local customs while overseas, and they expect foreigners will do likewise when visiting Taiwan.

First and foremost is the introduction. The Taiwanese are insular, literally, and they don't particularly appreciate surprise guests. Although they're quick on their commercial feet, they resent efforts to catch them off guard. Blustering business types arriving unexpectedly at offices demanding to see the "head honcho" will most likely end up speaking to someone in middle management (if anyone at all). And after such an inauspicious beginning, the project will be marked by a great disadvantage, regardless of its surface appeal.

A letter of introduction forwarded by either a Taiwanese intermediary or a foreign source known to your local contact will open doors for your company. This will serve as a form of *bona fides* and will give your counterpart some frame of reference. If you have difficulty securing such a letter, consider contacting the China External Trade Development Council (CETRA), a government service designed specifically to encourage business with Taiwan; it has offices in many major world cities. (Their website address is listed in Chapter 24.)

Family Ties

The Taiwanese prefer to do business with members of their immediate and extended family. They rely on relatives for advice and trust their judgment — so any previous connection with a Taiwanese (through work or even a college connection, in your home country or abroad) will greatly aid your dealings on the island. It doesn't matter if your "connection" doesn't work in a field related to your project, as long as he or she can vouch for your character. Character, after all, is what the Taiwanese will be looking for in the early stages of the project. Their business relationships, like their family relations, are assumed to be long-term, and good character is a prerequisite.

You'll often be asked about your own family. If you're married and have children, feel free to sing their praises; it isn't considered boorish. You may even be asked to display photographs, so be prepared. These inquiries are a means of assessing your character and aren't meant as attempts to "snoop" into your personal life. "Family" is equated with "stability," and a successful marriage with children shows an ability to commit. If you're single or divorced, downplay that fact and concentrate on your siblings and parents.

International Networking

The Taiwanese business world extends far beyond the island's borders. A reputation forged in Taipei will follow (or haunt) you throughout much of Asia and many parts of the U.S. or Europe. Mainland China, Singapore and Hong Kong have direct links to Taiwan (regardless of the political situation), while much of developing Asia depends on Taiwanese money to fuel growth. Like all good businesspeople, the Taiwanese like to work with a "known quantity," so you'll find that your success here can lead to bigger and better projects elsewhere. Similarly, failure or lack of follow-through will greatly decrease (or even eliminate) your access to Taiwan's extended business network. If ever there was a place where "your reputation precedes you," it's Sino-Asia.

9 Strategies for Success

Some Ground Rules

Every business culture has its particular ground rules. Taiwan's are similar to those of Hong Kong and Singapore but more advanced than those of mainland China. The Taiwanese have made a conscious effort to study the business habits of other countries and it would be to your advantage to learn to recognize the nuances at play.

1. Seek out introductions.

"Going it alone" is certainly within the realm of possibility, but, as previously discussed, you'll make the best use of your expensive overseas travel time by getting someone to introduce you *beforehand* to needed contacts. Taiwanese companies are distributed worldwide. Even if they're engaged in fields unrelated to your product or service, it's worth your while to express interest in the Taiwanese market to these domestic contacts over a business dinner. In return, they'll gain a good understanding of your business and advise you as to how your product or service will "play" in the Taiwanese marketplace. Most importantly, they may be willing to vouch for your character and business acumen.

2. Get "on the ground" experience.

A very common mistake novices make concerning Asia is traveling there filled with notions of closing deals on the first trip. It simply doesn't happen. Even with the very best contacts, you'll have to spend a great deal of time (and show considerable interest) in the target market before any deal will even be considered. Even major international corporations can spend years working on deals that might take weeks in the West. As a rule, the more development a market needs, the slower the pace. Still, Taiwan is much farther along than China or Vietnam, though decidedly slower than New York City or Munich.

3. Study the culture.

"Doing your homework" isn't a suggestion, it's a requirement. The Taiwanese view their present and their future in terms largely dictated by their lengthy past. Gaining a good overview of their history (see recommendations in Chapter 24) will go a long way toward getting you on the inside track. Besides gaining insights into your counterpart's psyche, you'll impress them with your knowledge and interest. It will also help you sort out any cultural biases (theirs or yours).

Foreigners conducting business here are expected to participate in important holiday celebrations, the Lunar New Year in particular. This means throwing employee banquets and giving annual bonuses and *hong bao* envelopes. Skimping or trying to downplay such traditions will only serve to undermine you. During Ghost Month (the seventh lunar month), some Sino-Taiwanese refrain from initiating new businesses, holding weddings, and other important undertakings.

4.   **Learn the language.**

If you have the wherewithal to take intensive language lessons, by all means do so. The Taiwanese take great pride in their language and are well aware of how difficult it is to learn. If you lack fluency, use a translator, but at least learn some basic phrases in *kuo-yu*. It's all part of showing your commitment to the Taiwanese marketplace. You may receive some good-natured ribbing about your pronunciation but take it in stride. Acceptance of their critiques will most likely lead to them asking for help with the pronunciation of *your* language — especially English.

5.   **Exhibit patience.**

In the West (the U.S. in particular), "flying off the handle" when displeased isn't considered unusual behavior. In Buddhist-based cultures, however, emotional outbursts are seen as a loss of control and a sign of unworthiness to lead. Patience is held in great esteem throughout Sino-Asia. If displeasure *must* be shown in public, it's done quietly and with a minimal loss of face to all involved.

Relations in Taiwan will require a great deal of nurturing, so be prepared to take a long-term view. If you're impatient by nature, send another representative from your company to lay the groundwork and reserve your visits for key decisions only. "Type A" personalities rarely experience success here, so keep them off of your negotiating team.

6.   **Learn to enjoy formality.**

Business meetings and dinner meetings are all somewhat stodgy affairs. The concept of "laid back" probably won't enter the Sino-Asian business lexicon anytime soon. If you can't thrive in a structured and formal atmosphere, Taiwan will be a very difficult market for you to crack.

But that's not to say that Taiwanese business-people aren't friendly. On the contrary they're enormously cordial. However, the Confucian hierarchy is always maintained. Bosses remain bosses and subordinates remain subordinates even at social functions. You may find yourself being deferred to in situations wherein you would normally let your sense of egalitarianism rule. Don't fight the current. Swim with it. It's thousands of years old and has swallowed many transgressors. Ignoring the hierarchical rules is a major faux pas and will be viewed as a form of uncouthness. Manners are *not* optional.

7. Leave your arrogance at home.

Humility is another virtue shared by Buddhist and Confucian philosophies alike. Arrogance is seen as a rather sizable character flaw and must be avoided at all costs. Flashy displays of wealth, intelligence or strength are taken as proof of an undeveloped soul and an immature personality, and they aren't considered desirable traits in a business partner. For the Buddhist, *The humble man has achieved everything worthwhile.*

8. Learn the value of face.

As mentioned, *mien-tzu* (face) is a very important concept in Asia. Everyone is responsible for maintaining their own *mien-tzu* as well as that those around them. Never openly criticize your counterparts, their subordinates or your team members. Most of all, don't do anything to disgrace yourself or you'll have breached the loyalty of your team. In Taiwan, "setbacks" are often permanent.

9. Downplay money.

The Taiwanese are extremely savvy, and they have a deep regard for profit. However, their culture demands that a business's primary goal be to serve the good of the whole group. Money will have little meaning if the relationship isn't "harmonious." (As will be discussed in Chapter 13, this harmony often comes at a high price.)

Whether you agree with their philosophy or not, be aware that talking about profit too early in the game will probably bring negotiations to a quick and permanent halt. Be patient, bide your time, and be clear about your requirements when the time comes.

10. Don't be afraid to ask for help.

All of the island's major cities have expatriate communities, often with members from your home country. Any hotel concierge or urban taxi driver can tell you where they congregate. There's no sense in reinventing the wheel. Seek out the counsel of those who've already succeeded here. They'll know whom you should talk to, whom you should avoid, and all of the unlisted phone numbers.

Expatriates love to hold forth on their experiences (good and bad), so be prepared for lengthy conversations. Try to get a broad a range of input, and don't take any one expat's word as gospel. It may cost you a few dollars worth of "entertainment fees" to get the information you need, but it may be the best investment you can make during your early stages of market investigation. You may be forging business and social relationships that will last a lifetime.

11. Don't assume confidentiality.

Business is highly competitive here and few things stay secret. Never take for granted that your telephone calls, faxes or correspondence are confidential, unless you specifically request that they remain so.

10 Time

Circular versus Linear

The Buddhist cultures that make up most of Sino-Asia view time in a circular pattern, suggesting a continuum that has no start or finish, no forward or backward. In contrast, Western culture has a tendency to view time in a linear fashion, with a clear starting point, forward movement and an endpoint. The Western fear of "wasting" time isn't an integral component of the Sino-Asian psyche.

The Taiwanese have a much more accommodating approach to time than mainland Chinese do. Through their expansive international business presence, the Taiwanese have adapted themselves to virtually every culture's concept of time. From Central America's *mañana* approach, to the U.S.'s fast-paced hustle, to Japan's just-in-time precision, Taiwan handles them all.

If you're buying, you'll get the product whenever and wherever you want it. Sellers, however, will move at their pace, which is in line with the Buddhist concept of the fluidity and endless supply of time. In other words, be prepared to wait.

Appointments

The Taiwanese have a modern and efficient business culture and they're well aware of the expenses incurred during foreign business trips. But airline costs, hotel bills, meals, ground transportation and translator fees are of little value if nobody shows up for your appointments. Let your contacts know where you'll be staying, so that they can leave messages for you regarding any schedule changes; you may wish to rent a cellular phone. It's advisable to verify your appointments and transportation reservations at least a day in advance.

Taiwanese businesspeople will make every effort to be punctual, but know that traffic is horrendous in larger cities. Keep a map handy when selecting meeting sites and accommodations. You may even wish to conduct meetings at your hotel, if suitable. Should your contacts miss an appointment, don't dismiss them out of hand as being disinterested. Keep in mind that business in Asia is conducted at all hours. Your overseas schedule can easily run 12 to 16 hours a day. Use lunches and dinners (even breakfast) to catch up on meetings.

If you're on a tight schedule, let your counterparts know in advance. Taiwanese often plan meals as part of meetings and it would be a major loss of face if you were to leave without dining. Giving them notice of your schedule will also allow them to plan their presentations and to pace the meeting. While they understand the Western preoccupation with time, the Taiwanese do not like to be rushed — especially when you're selling and they're buying. Schedule to the benefit of all the attendees and keep the primacy of the relationship in mind at all times.

11 Business Meetings

Choosing a Site

The Taiwanese observe the Golden Rule of Business: *The person with the gold makes the rules!* If you're visiting Taiwan to *sell* products, your company will be meeting wherever and whenever your contacts prefer. Though probably inconvenient for you, it's part of the Sino-Asian negotiating technique. Be prepared for a long, grueling day.

When you come to the island to *buy*, the Taiwanese will expect to accommodate your wishes. The level and professionalism of your requests will be seen as measures of your company's status and also of your personal *mien-tzu*. At some point in the negotiations, the Taiwanese will wish to show off their facilities, but the initial meeting should be made at a site of your choosing. Selecting your hotel can be risky, unless it's an impressive facility. Most Asian businesspeople measure the success of your company by the amount of money it spends on you. If you or your boss are pennypinchers when it comes to expense accounts, Asia will be a difficult place to make a good impression. The best way around this problem is to utilize a local business center or restaurant as a meeting site. Another choice might be to use the facility of a fellow expatriate. A last alternative would be for you to initiate the request to tour their facility.

If the purpose of your trip is to form a joint venture, it's best to let the Taiwanese choose the meeting facility — but maintain a veto. Since much of the discussion will involve the subject of ownership percentage, the Taiwanese (like many Asians) will seek to keep you off balance by making you uncomfortable. This will generally take the form of getting you as far away from your hotel (or airport) as possible. In their mind this will make you dependent on them and therefore more susceptible to their demands. While this technique sounds somewhat childish, it can be effective if you aren't prepared for it. Should they suddenly need to show you a facility 50 miles outside of Taipei, you may wish to decline for scheduling purposes. If not, make it clear that the tour must be brief and that serious negotiations will be put off for the duration. Take your own drivers and translators along for additional reassurance.

If *you* choose the site, make sure it's professionally outfitted. Either keep it simple or go way "over the top." Anything in between will most likely be seen as cheap, unprofessional, or both.

Preparation

Overseas business trips are expensive and meetings are their focal point, so if you're not going to do your homework, you might as well stay at home. Find out everything you can about the companies you'll be meeting with and the members of their delegations. Besides making basic financial information available, some companies issue picture books of their executives. Learning names and faces ahead of time will give you a leg up in discussions and will add face all around. (The Internet and CETRA can be very helpful in this area.)

Any materials you bring with you for distribution must be of professional quality. Photocopies of brochures and financial statements aren't acceptable. Don't ask your counterparts to make copies of your originals. Find out how many sets of presentation materials you'll need for all of your meetings and then double the number. Make sure to include a company profile along with detailed information about delegation members (background, education, job title and years with the company). Bind everything in company logo folders and ship them over to your hotel in advance via a reliable overnight shipper. Don't ship them through as luggage on your airline; arriving in Taiwan minus your presentation materials will limit your possibilities for success.

Paper or Plastic?

If you're planning to use your laptop for presentations, make sure that you or a member of your team is highly proficient in fixing hardware and software glitches. The malfunctioning laptop has replaced the slide projector as the modern-day enemy of presenters worldwide so come prepared with backup systems. Check with your Taiwanese hotel when making reservations to see if you'll need to bring voltage and modem converters from your home country.

If you're trying to avoid the high-tech route by using paper, make sure that your materials are in color where applicable (no bar charts in varying shades of gray, please) and printed on quality paper. Overhead projectors may be in order for presentations to large groups. (Reasonably sized and priced travel models are available for both transparencies and computers. You may find it easier to use a local supplier in Taiwan but make the arrangements well in advance of your arrival.)

Translated Materials

If you can afford to have all of your materials (including business cards) translated into *kuo-yu*, by all means do so. Have them checked by a native speaker; more than one traveler has been embarrassed by backward and upside-down characters. The vast majority of Taiwanese businesspeople speak English, so if you can't afford or secure Chinese translations, English will suffice. But German, Spanish, Italian, French or Hindi simply won't work.

When deciding what materials to share with your Taiwanese counterparts, keep in mind that intellectual property rights have only limited protection here. While Taiwan is trying to change its image as a prominent violator of copyright laws, the problem continues to exist.

Let the Meeting Begin

A second-in-command will introduce the Taiwanese delegation, moving from lowest to highest rank. Your team may wish to follow this same protocol to avoid confusion. Business cards are exchanged at this time and carefully read; bring lots of them and make sure every member of the Taiwanese delegation gets one. Don't rush this procedure or casually pocket a counterpart's card. Read each one carefully and don't put it away until the meeting is over.

Seating is dictated by hierarchy, with equal-ranking members of each delegation seated across from their counterparts. If your company is running the meeting make sure that your team and the meeting planner are aware of this important protocol. Seating your junior sales rep opposite the Taiwanese leader will only serve to confuse (or insult) the delegation.

Bring translators, even if the English skills of the Taiwanese team are quite proficient. When the going gets tricky, the Taiwanese will revert to Chinese among themselves. The presence of your translator will keep everything out in the open. He or she will also be useful when it comes to interpreting technical jargon. Translators should sit to the side and rear of the leaders of your team.

Chitchat and All That

Before getting down to business , small talk is in order. If the Taiwanese are running the meeting, the first- or second-in-command will issue a formal welcome on behalf of the company, the city and the country. Informal comments on the weather, local celebrations, international developments or economic conditions will ensue. The closing part of this welcome will deal with the hopes for a successful outcome to the meetings and wishes for a long-term and harmonious relationship. Although speaking to the whole group the host will most likely focus on the highest-ranking member of your team. Should your delegation be running the meeting, these same protocols should be observed.

When it's your turn to speak, reply with acceptance of the welcome and laudatory comments about your hosts and Taiwan in general. Keep references to the reason for your visit general, and avoid addressing the negotiations. List the accomplishments of your company in a matter-of-fact manner but don't appear boastful. The Taiwanese like to deal with successful companies but not those that think they're doing Taiwan a favor.

Breaking Bread, Cutting Deals

Depending on the timing of the meeting, food may be an integral part of the program. Taiwanese take great pride in lavishing their cuisine upon visitors. Meetings and tours scheduled near noon may be preceded by a four- or five-course meal. Dinner meetings may be conducted on company premises and involve ten to fifteen courses. Dining protocol will be taken up in Chapter 19, but some comments are due here.

The Taiwanese are quite knowledgeable about the world's cuisines and table manners, and they're very impressed when you show interest and acumen concerning theirs. Make sure every member of your team can use chopsticks (although forks may be offered). Chopstick usage, though a small point, is further proof that your group is interested and experienced in Sino-Asian cultures.

Don't fuss over what food you're willing to try, and put whatever diet you may be adhering to "on hold," if doing so won't endanger your health. The Taiwanese aren't likely to serve up their most exotic dishes early in your relationship but there may be some items you've never seen before. Try everything and compliment the preparation. You're here to make friends and to form a lasting relationship, so don't offend your hosts with your provincialism. Remember, the Taiwanese may find meatloaf about as appetizing as you find braised chicken feet.

Also, keep in mind that not everyone is cut out to work overseas. Brief potential team members about what to expect and make their inclusion on the trip contingent on their ability to "roll with the punches." Whiners with fussy table habits and cultural biases will do great damage to your project and are best left back at the home office.

Tea Time

Tea will be served most meetings. Coffee will be offered to Westerners and cool drinks provided if the weather dictates. Taiwan doesn't share the West's health concerns about caffeine, sugar and fat so refrain from asking for decaffinated coffee, low-fat milk or diet colas. Asking for something your host can't provide will cause embarrassment and a loss of *mien-tzu* for the both of you.

Endgame

It's the duty of the host to determine when the meeting (dining or not) has come to an end. The Taiwanese host will stand and make a brief statement about the content of the meeting and about future negotiations. Your team members should shake hands with their counterparts and then make an effort to do so with all other members of the host's team. Your team should depart the premises as a group if possible and avoid any discussion of the meeting until out of earshot of the hosts. Keep in mind that the drivers provided during your visit may be in the employ of your hosts and eager to overhear your comments.

If the meeting was the last in a series of successful negotiations, your hosts will most likely present your team with gifts. *This is not a form of bribery* but a manifestation of the "harmony" of your new relationship. Be prepared to reciprocate with distinctive, professional gifts from your home country. Pens, leather binders, team jackets and the like bearing your company logo and manufactured in your home market are the most appropriate.

12 Negotiating with Taiwanese

Taiwan shares many negotiating techniques with Hong Kong and mainland China. But unlike pre-1997 Hong Kong, Taiwan doesn't have a commercial legal structure based in British common law; Taiwanese contracts with foreign companies aren't nearly as binding. And unlike in mainland China, the Taiwanese don't approach business deals with a "take it or leave it" posture.

The island's colonial history has given its negotiators a respect for foreigners (read Westerners) that borders on a fear of "economic colonization." This, coupled with a very possible conflict with the mainland puts Taiwan in a serious dilemma. On the one hand, without the presence of extensive foreign investment on Taiwan, China would have no second thoughts about overrunning the island. On the other hand, too much foreign capital means giving up economic independence. Foreign negotiators must acknowledge this ambivalence towards external investment in order to be successful.

Turnabout is Fair Play

Negotiations will always be controlled by the party who's buying or, in the case of joint ventures, by the party putting up the most valuable assets. The Taiwanese will use modern contract negotiations coupled with long-standing Sino-Asian tactics to accomplish their ends.

The first day of negotiations will be filled with a great deal of harmonious talk and face building. Banquets, tours and smiles may cajole the visiting team into believing that all is going well. While this may be true, the negotiations have yet to begin in earnest. In reality, the Taiwanese are using this time to take the other side's measure and to seek out the weakest link in their team's position.

Under the guise of "special tours," your engineers or salespeople may be separated from the group and queried on a variety of topics. Visiting foreigners can overcome this divide-and-conquer technique by becoming extremely inquisitive during the "special tour." They may even wish to arrange preset questions for team members to ask. Turnabout is fairplay.

This early acclimation period also serves to "run out the clock" on your visit, thereby decreasing your ability to maneuver. (Thus, disclosure of your departure date or home-office deadline may be used against you.) If you're buying, insist on keeping this period to a minimum. If you're selling, then your team must bide its time, maintain a unified front, and wait for your hosts to get down to business.

Devilish Details

The Taiwanese have extensive technical prowess and a culture that worships bureaucracy — a dangerous combination that can stretch a one-hour meeting into days. Information from both sides of the table will be discussed and dissected in detail, then submitted for their team's consensus during recesses. After returning to the table, almost the exact same topics may come up for discussion and further review. Be patient. Whereas Westerners like to review the "upside" and the "downside" of an issue, the Taiwanese are quite happy to look at the same issue from every point on the compass. Consensus building and fear of missing an important detail drive their private discussions.

Taiwanese business leaders act as guides for decisions made by the group, and such decisions are never rushed into. Don't look for their leader to "take the bull by the horns," as is the Western style. Most likely the Taiwanese *have* the bull by the horns, the tail, as well as all four legs and are trying to determine what to let go of first. If you're buying or you're the potential majority partner in the deal, tolerate only as much side discussion and delay as courtesy requires. (Unlike the mainland Chinese, the Taiwanese don't labor under the illusion that they can have everything their way.) But take heart in the fact that once a decision has finally been made, implementation should proceed apace.

The Power of Contingency Plans

The Taiwanese will be looking for you to reveal plans early in the negotiations. This allows them to mold the deal to their greatest advantage. This ploy is best dealt with by either revealing your position incrementally or by arriving at the negotiating table with numerous options already planned out in detail. This second approach — responding to their requests with complex options rather than a simple "yes" or "no" — will disarm the Taiwanese. They won't wish to appear to be unprepared or unknowledgeable and will become more amenable to your original proposal. This stratagem must be worked out well in advance of the negotiations, with options and fall-back positions discussed in detail.

Keep Records

Your counterparts will be keeping track of everything you and your team members say (even at dinner), looking for inconsistencies and statements favorable to their position. These may be hurled back at you during negotiations, so be prepared. When caught in their own words, Chinese speakers often offer up "poor translation" as the excuse. Feel free to do the same. The best defense, however, is a well-briefed team and a consistent position. Another countermeasure is to appoint a member of your team as a recordkeeper and review the notes after each meeting. You're a long way from home and playing for big money, so keep good records.

When Things Bog Down

Many foreigners find the Taiwanese take on a haughty demeanor when negotiations start to bog down. This isn't a sign that they're demonstrating a sense of superiority; if anything, it's the opposite. The Taiwanese team is likely covering their lack of strength (and perhaps even their lack of knowledge about the topic under discussion).

This stance is the result of a long history of colonization and foreign domination. The fear of once again being bested by foreigners is omnipresent. The Taiwanese have seen the rest of the world and realize they have a lot to learn, and they fear a public display of their shortcomings — a response that's easily assuaged . . . or exploited.

Accountability

One of the mistakes foreign companies make in Asia is not negotiating the accounting rules as part of the regular contract. (In mid-1997, a Taiwanese bank was ordered to pay fines of US$22 million and to forfeit its profits, for failing to accurately report its purchase of Chinese American Bank in New York.) Taiwan would like to become a member of the World Trade Organization, but as this hasn't happened yet, it's not bound by the rules set forth in the GAAP (Generally Accepted Accounting Principles). Be sure to negotiate an accounting system that's consistent with your home office and domestic tax law.

For the most part, contracts signed in Taiwan are enforceable in Mandarin, the language of the government. The contract will be translated for your convenience, but the translation will have no bearing on the court's interpretation. Always insist that the final Mandarin contract be given to you for review overnight. Sign nothing until you and your translator have thoroughly dissected every aspect of it. Along with the main body of the deal, make sure the accounting standards and profit repatriation guarantees are included and worded to your satisfaction.

The Price of Harmony

Sino-Asian businesspeople have a standard practice of delivering any bad news late in the game. You'll be able to tell that the "downside" is on its way when your counterparts start reiterating the need for the preservation of harmony. The bad news is generally delivered by a second-in-command (in order to save the leader's *mien-tzu)* and will be phrased in such a way that the whole group will seem to be absorbing the brunt. Rest assured that only your side will suffer.

Having maintained your composure in a suitably Confucian manner up until this point, it's time to show your displeasure. Let it be known that you feel the withholding of this new information was deliberately deceptive (which it was) and not in keeping with the harmonious relationship on the table. You may even wish to give the appearance that the negotiations are now at an end.

Often this bad news takes the form of some local building code or tax; your counterparts will plead that it's out of their control. Don't relent. Inform them that it was their responsibility to know such details in advance. Their position relies on your passivity and acceptance; by accusing them of violating the relationship, you'll put them on the defensive. In most cases, the obstacle will miraculously evaporate. At the very least, the burden of fixing the problem has been shifted to the Taiwanese.

There's a viable defense that your team can use to prevent this form of manipulation. Throughout the negotiations, ask constantly if there are any possible problems or obstacles that would get in the way of a harmonious and profitable completion of the deal. Make it clear that they're responsible for knowing the legal and tax structure of their own country. You may even wish to insert language in the contract protecting your right to renegotiate should "unforeseen" circumstances or codes threaten the success of the deal.

Playing the Barbarian

Being a *gwielo* has its advantages. If you're a Westerner, it will be assumed that you're impatient and given to emotional outbursts. You may wish to reserve such stereotypical behavior for just the right moment. If you remain patient throughout the negotiations, it will be difficult for your counterparts to read your tactics, and they'll believe that they've lulled you into doing things the Taiwanese way.

Then, if negotiations start to bog down or if the Taiwanese become too demanding, inject some Western-style confrontation to the proceedings. Your movement between styles will keep them off balance and disrupt their plans. It is advisable to use this methodology *only* if it appears that your team is being manipulated toward an unfavorable position. For the most part, the Taiwanese are very professional in their dealings with foreigners and will only use those tactics deemed necessary to close a deal.

There's No "No" There

Many foreigners leave the negotiating table believing that although things didn't go perfectly, success is still possible. They're wrong. Courtesy dictates that the Taiwanese not come right out and say "no" to your proposal. (However, this courtesy doesn't extend to bureaucrats and police officers, who have no problem with the word.)

You can save yourself a lot of time and money by understanding that the negotiations are over and it's time to move on when:

1. Important members of the Taiwanese delegation are suddenly called away from or can't attend the meetings,

2. You're referred to a technical department for your presentation,

3. Your Taiwanese counterparts stop asking questions about your product or proposal, or

4. The Taiwanese ask that they be given a lengthy period of time in which to consider or research your proposal.

Translators: Not a Luxury

As mentioned earlier, regardless of Taiwanese English skills, it's advisable to have a translator with you at all meetings — for a number of reasons.

First, the translator can clarify cultural nuances or protocols that may escape your notice. Secondly, the Taiwanese are apt to speak to each other in Mandarin or Fukienese when they wish to keep your team in the dark. Having a translator present will reduce the effectiveness of this strategy. Thirdly, although the meeting will most likely be conducted in English, some technical terms may require definition. Lastly, because the contract enforcement will be in Mandarin, your translator will be key in making sure that the deal is written as agreed.

The following tips will aid in your selection:

- **Hire your own.** Don't use an interpreter supplied by your Taiwanese counterpart. Besides not looking out for your best interests, they will be reporting to the Taiwanese on everything they overhear. The optimal situation would be for you to bring an interpreter from your home country at your company's expense. If you have to make the choice between including an extra staff member or a translator on your overseas team, go with the translator.

- **Keep the translator close at hand.** If you're hiring a translator in Taiwan (your hotel can assist you), make sure that there's ample time to brief him (or her) before negotiations begin. Besides knowing your company's products, he must be familiar with your speech patterns. At the end of each day review the day's events and prepare for the next round of negotiations. Avoid letting your translator get separated from your team, if possible, as he may be approached by the Taiwanese with requests for inside information.

- **Keep it simple.** If you must use a locally hired interpreter, make it as easy for him as possible. Use complex terminology only when absolutely necessary, and avoid everything but the most general type of humor (jokes do not translate well). Keep your sentences short and pause often, so that the translator can interpret as few points as possible at one time. When speaking, focus your eyes on your counterparts; don't look at the translator. The Taiwanese will be interpreting your body language on their own.

- **Treat them well.** Your translator should be well-paid, well-fed, well-rested and generally treated with respect. Translators can be a great hindrance if their loyalty waivers, and you may not be able to detect their treachery. Give them a substantial tip or gift at the completion of the negotiations to ensure their confidentiality once you leave Taiwan.

Contracts, Taiwanese Style

Perhaps more than any other Chinese group, the Taiwanese are experienced with a foreigner's need for detailed, enforceable contracts. Lawyers are rarely invited to participate in negotiations, so don't expect (or demand) too much legal wrangling. Still, the "relationship" will always supersede the contract, and disputes will be negotiated, not litigated. If you accept this fact, your deals will run much more smoothly and prosperously.

 Business Outside the Law

Underground Economy

In Taiwan, the underground and the main-stream exist in parallel, without necessarily conflicting. What's unique to Sino-Asia is the willingness to *admit* to underworld connections. This attitude dates back to imperial China, when the Triads (secret societies that extorted "protection" monies) acted as a form of "people's government," since the emperor offered the average citizen little legal protection. Even before arriving in Taiwan in 1949, the KMT had established close ties with the Green Gang, a triad that had helped overthrow the Qing dynasty.

Today, drug trafficking, extortion, kidnapping, gambling, prostitution and bribery all flourish (along with the sale of fake "Rolexes," pirated music tapes, and the like). Taipei's liberalization, designed as a bulwark against Beijing's threats, was put in place to win the favor of Western governments. The net result has been a lessening of police power and a significant drop in both private investment and GNP growth. Meanwhile, a government crack-down has indicted or investigated thousands of corruption cases since mid-1996 and introduced Asia's first anti-money-laundering bill.

Palm Grease a.k.a. Tea Money

Don't be surprised if hints about bribery are dropped by business associates — especially if your deal requires some form of political clearance or governmental licensing. This is considered by locals to be just another form of taxation. Foreigners must weigh the political and legal ramifications for themselves. U.S. citizens working abroad are bound by the Foreign Corrupt Practices Act, which makes bribery a felony; many other countries allow such activity as a legitimate (and deductible) expense.

Regardless of your moral or legal parameters, keep in mind that the payment of one bribe will be followed by the request for another and that bribery is technically illegal in Taiwan. Backing out of a deal after a bribe has been paid may result in your arrest for "attempting" to bribe a public official, and the threat of this action may be applied to the negotiations in order to keep you at the table.

A New Take on Taxes

Like businesspeople the world over, the Taiwanese often keep two sets of books in order to avoid paying their full share of taxes. In a creative effort to remedy this, the government established a lottery known as *Tung Yi Fa Pyau* (Unified Invoice System). Businesses are now required to purchase a monthly booklet of numbered invoices, and the receipts from these enter a monthly grand prize drawing.

Black Market Economics

Many criminals have interests in legitimate businesses, including transportation, construction, entertainment, and retail, and foreign businesspeople will likely end up dealing with some element of this overlap. As long as your parts of the deal are legitimate, there's little to worry about.

If you get involved with the wrong sorts and push comes to shove on a business deal, there'll be little compunction about bringing some rather unsavory forces to bear. Looking for help from the Taiwanese government will probably be fruitless. The Triads are endemic in Asia, and they have a great deal of influence in the U. S. and Europe. Perform a thorough "due diligence" before signing anything.

14 Names & Greetings

The Twain Sometimes Meet

The Taiwanese approach to their names further exhibits their desire to match tradition to the modernity of a much larger world. Most use the traditional Chinese system of family name first, followed by middle and given names, but they realize that these are often mispronounced by foreigners.

It's very common for Taiwanese males to introduce themselves in English, using the initials of their given names followed by a simplified version of their family name. When traveling overseas Chiang Teng-kuo becomes "T. K. Chang." Taiwanese women often adopt an English first name (e.g., *Jasmine* or *Pearl*) to be applied before the family name. Women aren't required to take their husband's name when they marry, but many will adopt it while traveling overseas.

Many younger Taiwanese (usually the progeny of those who've had extended overseas educational or business assignments) were given non-Chinese surnames at birth. Chosen for their distinctive sound (e.g., *Cedric* or *Eloise*), many of these may have fallen out of general use in the West. Whatever name or initials they choose to give you, respect their wishes. Don't commit the faux pas of asking Cedric what his "real" name is.

Family names in Chinese culture are few in number relative to the size of the entire Sino-Asian population. This isn't due to a lack of creativity but rather is symptomatic of the strength of family ties. Many companies and political organizations are structured around bloodlines. *Wong's, Chan's* and *Yung's* abound on Taiwan, and you may cause general chaos if you arrive at a company asking to speak to "Mr. Lee."

It's best to ask for someone by their full name and to include their job title. If you can present the business card of the person you're scheduled to meet to the receptionist, it will make everyone's job easier.

Business Cards

Although many wealthy businesspeople in the West shun the idea of exchanging business cards, especially with lower ranking individuals, it's standard practice in Taiwan. To *not* present a card is a sign of unpreparedness, even rudeness. Make sure you bring lots of them (as in hundreds), even for a short stay. Always present them with both hands and with the lettering facing the recipient.

It's always best to translate your cards into Mandarin, and have this checked by a native speaker before printing; a poor translation will do more harm than good. Don't attempt to translate logo names, but do pay special attention to job titles and service descriptions. If you can't locate a Mandarin translation service in your home country, at least make sure that your card is translated into English. Your efforts will be appreciated.

Chops

The personalized signature seal, known as a "chop" or *jang,* is a holdover from a time when many Chinese were incapable of using the complex characters of their printed language (and finger-printing and photo IDs had yet to be invented). A chop consists of a short block of stone or wood with the symbol for the holder's name carved into the bottom end and often a decorative animal (possibly one's zodiac sign) carved into the top. For signing, the bottom is pressed into a thick red paste.

While illiteracy is now almost nonexistent here, chops are still used for "signing" most official documents (as well as works of art). Government papers, contracts and deeds all require them, as do Taiwanese banks when accessing an account or a safety deposit box. (International banks accept conventional identification.)

Make sure you get a good Mandarin translation of your name before having it carved. Many a *gwielo* has been victimized by a chop carver who decided to take liberties with the translation. Take a Taiwanese friend with you when chop shopping just to be sure.

If your company maintains offices in Taiwan, refrain from displaying a chop on your desk if it's made of cheap materials (plastic or bamboo). Jade, ivory and even precious metals are *de rigueur* for display models. Some are available in custom-made satin-lined boxes covered with brocade. And always remember that chops "sign" your name to binding contracts, so maintain a reasonable level of security.

Terms of Respect

Most business with foreigners is conducted in English (usually fluently) and company-related titles are rarely included in the conversation once introductions have been made. Unlike mainland Chinese, the Taiwanese aren't obsessed with having their hierarchy reinforced at every turn.

Unless you're fluent in *kuo-yu*, it's not really necessary for you to observe the age-related terms of respect (such as *Lao*, Honorable Older One) that the Taiwanese use among themselves. The use of *Mr.*, *Miss*, *Madam* or *Mrs.* is acceptable. *Ms.* tends to create confusion if the listener isn't fluent in English. *Doctor* is widely used when addressing those who have achieved doctoral degrees; it's not reserved for physicians.

It's considered rude to address someone by their given name until a friendship has developed. The Taiwanese are quite forgiving on this point (especially of the overly familiar Americans), but you can show your good taste by referring to "Dr. Lee" at meetings until you're both ready for you to call him "Cedric." Your courtesy will be noted.

Handshakes

Because touching in public is a rarity except among the dearest of friends, handshakes are kept as brief as possible. Westerners, especially burly types, may find the Taiwanese handshake a bit on the limp side. This isn't an expression of weakness or passivity. Some older Taiwanese will actually use a two-handed version, with the left hand placed lightly on top of the handshake. Putting a vice-grip on your Taiwanese associate's hand will only serve to reinforce the image of you as a Western barbarian. Holding onto a woman's hand for more than the briefest moment will be considered rather forward.

Communication Styles

For all of their world travels, the Taiwanese remain very conservative and traditional, steeped in the *Analects* of Confucius (who, it's worth noting, received little recognition during his lifetime).

Mien-tzu versus "Thinking On One's Feet"

Maintaining harmony and balance is an obsession, both in social and commercial relationships. Meeting problems "head on" isn't considered to be a viable method of resolution. As problems arise, the Taiwanese will avoid addressing the issue through either silence or a change of subject. Any attempt to raise the subject again will meet with a similar response.

The goal is to resolve the problem in a more private fashion. Negotiations often take place behind-the-scenes, thus maintaining *mien-tzu* for all parties concerned. Don't press for a quick resolution unless it's a large problem that requires (in your mind at least) immediate attention. Although your culture may appreciate people who can "think on their feet," the Taiwanese don't. They act by consensus and should be allowed time to do so.

Look into the Empty Spaces

*It is enough that the language one uses gets
the point across.* – Confucius

The Taiwanese are very thrifty when it comes
to dispensing information. This isn't necessarily a
form of duplicity, though sometimes foreigners
may be tempted to interpret it that way. Their reti-
cence can have several motivations. When the news
is bad, they're striving to keep the damage (and
loss of face) to a minimum. When the news is good,
they're attempting to maintain a humble attitude
toward good fortune.

Either way, the information will be forthcoming
in due time. In the last case, you can be assured that
the less information you receive, the weaker your
counterpart's position. Silence or distraction are
often used to cover a tenuous position. Rather than
admit that their technical knowledge or financial
abilities are wanting, Taiwanese will hope that you'll
interpret silence as "keeping an ace in the hole."
Don't be fooled — if they had a stronger suit, they
would have played it at the opportunity.

Strangers & Foreigners

The Taiwanese can be exceedingly cordial with
people they know and with those they wish to
impress. However, anyone who has walked the
streets of Taipei can attest to the fact that strangers
are treated with brusqueness and indifference. This
behavior is sometimes attributed to overcrowding,
but it also exists in the countryside. It stems from the
nature of the relationship or lack thereof. If the Taiwanese have no relationship with you or any need to
form one, they won't invest time in courteous niceties. Be assured that it has little to do with racial or
cultural bias, nor is it a prelude to confrontation.
They treat their fellow countrymen in much the
same fashion.

Take their indifference in stride and don't expect your smiles to be returned. And don't be surprised if the stranger who jostled you at the airport this morning is brimming with cordiality tomorrow when you meet him for business. He'll never acknowledge having seen you the day before or apologize . . . too much loss of face!

Tips for Foreigners

To ensure that you're taken seriously and treated well, consider the following:

- **Maintain Dignity.** The Taiwanese don't see their country as a playground to be exploited by foreigners. It's possible to have fun and maintain your dignity at the same time. Causing a loss of face for yourself will cause your hosts to suffer a similar loss.

- **Avoid Arrogance.** Boisterous and arrogant behavior is interpreted as a lack of humility and self-control. Humility and self-deprecation are the rule. Confucius was clear on the point: *A gentleman is conscious of his own superiority without being contentious.*

- **Be Patient.** Taiwan will move at its own pace, regardless of the consequences. It's decades ahead of the mainland when it comes to getting things done, but it's not Tokyo or New York. Your impatience will motivate no one and will most likely be used against you. And under no circumstances should you exhibit it with bureaucrats or the police.
  (For more on this, see Chapter 18.)

 Customs

The Significance of Numbers

Numbers play a large role in Taiwanese day-to-day life. Some are considered lucky or evil, others derive their meaning from merely *sounding* like another word. Addresses are altered, license plates chosen, and company names and wedding dates selected on the basis of numerology. A child's name may be chosen according to the strokes a fortune-teller says the Chinese characters should contain.

Here are a few of the more significant numerological meanings:

- **Four (*Si*).** Sounds like the Chinese word for "death" and is therefore avoided in company names and as a floor designation in buildings. Gifts given in groups of four are considered a particularly bad omen.

- **Six (*Lin*).** Represents the six Chinese elements of nature (wind, mountain, river, lightning, moon and sun) and is a very lucky number.

- **Eight (*Ba*).** Sounds like the Chinese word for "prosperity" and so is a favorite for inclusion in a business address.

- **Thirteen (*Shi san*).** Has the same unlucky status as in Western cultures.

Lunar New Year

Also known as the Spring Festival or Chinese New Year, this is the country's biggest holiday. Many Taiwanese use it to mark a secondary birthday, which technically falls on the first moon of the first month. This new year/birthday celebration goes on for a minimum of three days.

New clothes are worn, the previous year's debts are paid off, ancestors are remembered, and relatives pay visits. The Chinese character *chwun* (springtime), printed on red paper, is pasted upside-down on the walls of homes and offices because the Chinese phrase "Spring turned upside-down" sounds similar to "Spring is here." Lots of family games are played, firecrackers are exploded in massive numbers, gifts are distributed, and many companies pay double wages or large yearly bonuses. *Hong bao* (small red envelopes) containing paper money — in even amounts and preferably with sequential serial numbers — are given to children and service personnel.

Holiday banquets usually feature fish — because *yu* (fish) sounds like *yu* (surplus), in other words, prosperity. To be invited to one of these dinners is a great honor. On the new year's second day, it's traditional for wives to visit their parents and other birth relatives. This custom dates back to a time when wives were the "property" of their husbands and often the target of spiteful mothers-in-law. This was a wife's one day of respite.

Very little work gets done in Taiwan a week before and the week after. Visitors can probably forget about hotel and airline reservations if they haven't made them a year in advance, and be aware that rates can be double or triple, as many Taiwanese living abroad choose this time to reunite with family and friends.

The last day of this festival is marked by the Lantern Festival. In ancient times, unchaperoned maidens carried paper lanterns out into the night, to the delight of prospective suitors. Today, battery-operated plastic lamps are ubiquitous, carried by children and teenagers of both sexes.

Gift Giving

In Taiwan, gifts express the desire for a prosperous future, reinforce a friendship, and show appreciation for a favor or a job well done. Westerners sometimes feel they're being given a bribe or being pressured for one. This is decidedly not the case. However, it's a very good idea for businesspeople to bring gifts from their home country.

Both Buddhism and Confucianism require a charitable and ungreedy approach to material goods. In fact, the Taiwanese show as much reluctance toward receiving a gift as they exhibit enthusiasm for giving one. Here are some guidelines:

- Always give and receive gifts with both hands, preferably palms up. This custom stems from ancient times, when an unseen hand might harbor a weapon. The meaning, therefore, is that the giver has no hidden agenda.

- Be careful to match your counterpart's gift in value so that proper levels of face will be maintained.

- Gifts to avoid include clocks and watches (death auguries), knives and scissors (they suggest a severed relationship), and towels and handkerchiefs (associated with funerals and sadness).

- When you're giving business gifts to groups, make sure that they reflect a hierarchy. Gifts bearing your company logo will be appreciated, especially if they're international brands.

- Gifts should be wrapped in red, gold, pink or yellow, as these are auspicious colors. White and black are reserved for funerals.

- Although the Taiwanese may go through a ritual of refusing your gift two or three times before accepting, it's not necessary for you to do the same. When presenting *your* gift, be persistent.

- Gifts are accepted humbly and aren't unwrapped in front of the giver. This saves face all around. If the receiver is disappointed and lets it show, he or she loses face. If the gift outshines other gifts received, the others lose face.

Weddings (Red) & Funerals (White)

Securing a good husband or wife is considered of primary importance (divorce is a taboo subject), and some marriages are arranged by professional matchmakers. Though mainland Communists tried to downplay and even ban elaborate weddings, Taiwan has elevated them to an art form.

Red, an auspicious color, is used for wedding invitations (called *syi jyou*, literally, joyful wine). Don't even *consider* declining one; it's virtually a cultural subpoena. There's only one item in the bridal registry — CASH — enclosed in a red envelope. A standard gift is NT$1000 (US$38), twice that if you attend with a spouse. (Never give NT$400 or NT$4000; the number 4 is taboo.) Closer friends, relatives and business partners are expected to give much more (3 to 4 times more). Since much of the cash is used to defray the cost of the banquet (the groom's family pays), include additional money for any friends or spouses in attendance. If you can't attend, you'll still be expected to send the money.

Wedding banquets can be lengthy, with ten-course meals and numerous toasts. If you are the employer of either the bride or the groom, you may be given a place of honor.

A funeral invitation (in a white envelope) also involves an outlay of cash. Once again, the going rate is NT$1000 and should be sent (again, in a white envelope) regardless of your ability to actually attend the ceremony. Like weddings, funerals can only be performed on days with lunar and numerological significance, possibly even weeks or months after the actual demise.

White robes and hoods are donned by close relatives, other attendees are expected to wear black. The tone of the event can run from solemn to nearly raucous — there've been reports of ceremonies that included strippers or young girls in bikinis singing songs to entertain the dead. All events will entail a great deal of wailing, often amplified by professional mourners. Gifts of cigarettes, liquor and food are proffered at makeshift altars.

Be prepared for a great deal of noise at the burial site as evil spirits are driven away. A banquet will ensue for friends and relatives, followed by a seven-week mourning period (during which brightly colored clothes are eschued). Then, offerings such as spirit money, paper clothes — even paper Mercedes (complete with mobile telephones) and paper houses (complete with servants) if the deceased was wealthy — are burned, so that the departed can enjoy these in the afterlife.

17 | Dress & Appearance

You Are What You Wear

The Taiwanese have cosmopolitan tastes and economic clout, and urban centers here are inhabited by the well heeled. Unlike on the mainland, where the *nouveau riche* are keen to display their wealth, the Taiwanese maintain a much more conservative approach. Finely tailored suits of dark blue and gray are worn by businessmen, generally with white, starched shirts and discreet neckwear. Their European-style shoes are always in high polish and good repair. Jewelry is expensive but tasteful.

Foreigners will be judged by their attire and grooming and treated accordingly. The Taiwanese assume that if you're visiting their country for either business or pleasure, you can't possibly be poor. Shabby clothes (like cut-offs and T-shirts) will be interpreted as a sign that you find their country unworthy of proper dress. You'll be tolerated but not respected, and many doors will remain closed.

You may find people paying a great deal of attention to your shoes and watches (no $5 digitals, please), so bring your best. Since you may have to take your shoes off in public, keep your socks clean and free of holes. Casual wear for men should be namebrand and always ironed. Lastly, gentlemen, if you wear an earring, it should be left on your dresser back home. Only pirates wear them in these waters.

Businesswomen should adopt a conservative and modest approach. Tailored suits of various weights should be worn throughout the year. Red should be avoided as the dominant color, as should black or white, due to their cultural significance. Jewelry and hairstyles should be discreet; 15 earrings and canary-yellow hair will only make the Taiwanese think that you're not to be taken seriously. Keep your skirt lengths modest and your necklines high. Western women have a reputation for being far less modest than Taiwanese women, and you do not need to attract any unwanted attention.

Casual Attire

Company-logo golf shirts are worn on hot days and are considered welcomed gifts. Shorts of reasonable length are acceptable for hot weather, but gym shorts are considered in poor taste on golf courses and in some restaurants (you may be refused service). Sandals, but not thongs, are accepted for outdoor use. If you bring athletic shoes or golf shoes make sure they're in good repair.

Modesty is also the order of the day for women. It can get hot and humid in Taiwan, but this isn't St. Tropez. Shorts, tops, tennis dresses and bathing suits should all be selected with a conservative eye. This is a very modest part of the world, so maintain your dignity at all times. There are no second chances.

Reading the Taiwanese

The Mechanics of Conversation

The Taiwanese, like many Asians, are often accused of being "inscrutable." This tired old stereotype is usually trotted out by Westerners who thrive on the allegedly "open" and "transparent" attitudes of their homelands.

One reason for this is that the Taiwanese don't view conversation as a competition sport premised on who-knows-the-most. For them, conversation is the beginning and continuance of a harmony wherein each party draws out what they need and contributes what's needed by others. Consequently, they'll often tell you what they believe you wish to hear. Two different answers to the same question are given not to preserve ambiguity but as a response to a perceived change of "need." In short, the truth is subject to the demands of harmony.

Here are some hints on the Taiwanese approach:

- Eye contact is kept to a minimum as a sign of respect. The Taiwanese don't value "looking someone straight in the eye"; any attempt to "stare down" an opponent during negotiations will only serve to convince the Taiwanese that you're mentally unstable.

- The Taiwanese often maintain a dour expression during serious discussions. This indicates neither displeasure, boredom nor lack of understanding; it's a way of keeping emotions in check while important decisions are being formulated.

- The concept of "in your face" doesn't exist for any but the crudest people in Taiwan. "Personal space" is respected, and people stand somewhat farther apart from each other when conversing than in the West.

- Smiling can mean pleasure, understanding or agreement, but it can also mean displeasure, confusion or disagreement. How will you know? Make sure everything is confirmed three or four times and explain things repeatedly.

- *Yes* means "We're thinking about it" and *no* is never used. Businesspeople will cancel meetings repeatedly rather than say the "n" word.

- The Taiwanese enjoy a good laugh as much as anyone but rarely when doing business. Forget about "inside" jokes, mild "ribbing" or puns. The Taiwanese have little experience with these, and they may begin to feel that you're taking advantage of their good nature.

- Be prepared for direct questions like "How old are you?," "Are you married?," "What's your salary?" or "How much did you pay for that watch?" The Taiwanese are trying to get a "fix" on your status, and therefore on how to address you. Still, overall, the Taiwanese prefer the circuitous route in conversation, as it allows them to preserve harmony.

- Don't hook your index finger when trying to beckon someone. Extend your arm, palm down, and move your fingers toward you.

- If a Taiwanese scratches his index finger up and down on his cheek, he probably means that someone has lost face.

- Touching is rare in public, so avoid hugs, pats on the back, or the collegial hand on the shoulder. When you've been accepted as a friend, the Taiwanese will let you know by lightly touching your arm. This is a very warm gesture and an honor, so never back away.

- The obscene Western gesture of holding up one's middle finger isn't understood here. If someone holds up a fist and draws his index finger as if pulling a trigger, it means that something is finished or someone's dead.

- To indicate the number ten, cross your index fingers; holding up all ten fingers will not be understood. For "no," move your hand from side to side, palm down.

- Balance is a significant aspect of Buddhist thought, and posture is an indication of intelligence and breeding. Slumping in a chair or slouching as you walk are seen as indications that you lack self-control and therefore must lead a woeful life. (Even melancholy teenagers maintain ramrod posture while sitting or bike riding.) Don't be surprised if a friend discreetly offers the services of an acupuncturist as a cure for your "woes."

19 Entertaining

Food: A Point of Pride

Taiwan has a genius for (some say an obsession with) food. Acquaintances greet each other not with inquiries about health or family but with *Ni chr bau le ma?* (Have you eaten yet?). Food quality is of the highest order. Popular dishes include squid with celery, clams with garlic, stuffed bean curd, three-cup chicken, omelettes with oysters or preserved radish, and fish-flavored eggplant.

Very few animals, sea creatures or plants are denied access to the *wok*. You may be offered tiger, python, turtle, bear paws (endangered, expensive, and reputedly high in vitamins and minerals), snake, roasted sparrows, jellyfish, pig trotters, braised ox phallus, "thousand-year-old" eggs, and, if you have a cold, dog (called *syang rou* or "fragrant meat," it's technically illegal). Vegetables may seem equally exotic, especially once sea cucumber and black fungus enter the menu. If you turn these down, your host will understand, but an adventuresome palate will greatly endear you. Telling your Taiwanese hosts that you enjoy their food will draw the same reaction as telling them that they have beautiful, intelligent children.

Business Dining

Dinner banquets are a very important part of business and should be attended at all costs. Be prepared for a lavish ten-course meal. (If your time in Taiwan permits, it will be in your best interest to invite your counterparts to a banquet of your own. And if you operate on the island on a permanent or regular basis, it's mandatory.)

Some larger Taiwanese companies have dining facilities on their premises with full-time chefs. The standard setup is for large round tables, with as many as twenty chairs to a table. The Taiwanese prefer that their counterparts be seated opposite them rather than adjacent. Hosts will generally try to be seated with their backs to a door — for the same reason that gifts are presented with two hands, as a way of demonstrating that there's no hidden agenda (or assassins lurking, as in ancient times). Allow the hosts to arrange the seating, as it assists in their concept of hierarchy; seating is especially important for banquets held to celebrate the closing of a deal.

Chopsticks & Table Protocol

The Taiwanese will see your adeptness at using chopsticks as an appreciation of their culture. Picking up the smallest morsels from serving dishes will bring endless (though seemingly patronizing) praise. (Note: For a clever gift, have quality chopsticks imprinted with your company's logo.)

Individual rice bowls are used to contain both rice and entrees. Serving dishes will be placed on a rotating tray (a large Lazy Susan) in the center of the table. Don't help yourself until the host has begun, and don't take items directly from the serving dish to your mouth. Also, try to be accepting if something is forced onto your plate.

Hold the rice bowl close to your face and, to some degree, push the food into your mouth. Fish bones or gristle can be removed from your mouth with the chopsticks and piled on a side dish or directly on the table. Don't put them back on your plate. *Never* stick the chopsticks in the rice bowl with the ends sticking straight up in the air, as this is reminiscent of funereal incense sticks and is considered very bad luck.

Men and women alike will belch (a sign of enjoyment) and pick their teeth at the table, though they'll cover their mouths for the latter. Many Taiwanese chew with their mouths open and speak at the same time. Though not visually pleasing, it can be taken as a sign of the festive nature of the dinner.

Dietary Restrictions

Because of the prevalence of Buddhism, vegetarianism is widely practiced. Don't be shocked when you see restaurants displaying what appears to be a swastika; this ancient Buddhist symbol designates vegetarian restaurants and food products that don't contain animal fat. Learning the phrase *Wo chi su* (I'm a vegetarian) will open some memorable dining experiences, as Taiwan has had many centuries to develop its recipes.

As there's no major Islamic or Jewish presence on the island, pork dishes are readily available, but feel free to turn them down. Salt and monosodium glutamate are standard ingredients in sauces. If you don't let your host know ahead of time about your restrictions on the latter two, there may be nothing for you to eat at the banquet except plain rice — and a great deal of *mien tzu* will be lost.

Toasting

Toasts are a big part of every banquet. But be forewarned: *Toasting is only done between equals.* Part of the rationale behind seating arrangements is to ensure that counterparts of equal rank are placed opposite each other. Only group leaders should toast the attendees as a whole. It's a major faux pas for a subordinate to toast anyone other than his or her designated opposite. A standard toast (a challenge, actually) is *gan pei* (dry glass). Accept at your own peril, as the challenges will get larger.

Dinner in a Private Home

Being invited to someone's home for dinner (called *wan fan* or "late rice") is an honor rarely extended to foreigners and should never be turned down. Arrive on time (never early) and be prepared to remove your shoes upon entering. Thong-type slippers will be provided (though with a limited size selection). Bringing a small gift is always acceptable, but it shouldn't be any form of food, as this might be taken be suggest that your host can't provide a meal. You'll be introduced to the entire family, which may extend through great grandparents.

Allow yourself to be seated at a place of honor. Your host will start by offering you each dish. Guest are always served first to assure that they're satisfied.

Many of the dishes will be family or regional specialties that the women of the house may have spent the entire day preparing. Try everything and comment on its fine quality. Turning something down or showing displeasure may deeply insult a member of the household.

Socializing

The Taiwanese work very hard and match that ardor when it's time to play. After-hours socializing is part and parcel of work. If you're visiting on business and the dinner meeting has been completed, you'll most likely be asked to join in some late-night socializing.

Drinking & Smoking

Alcohol and tobacco fuel Taiwan's nightlife. If you happen to be a particularly large Western male, you'll find many Taiwanese trying to "drink you under the table," in which case your best ploy is to let them think you're not up to it. Avoid *hua jiu quan* (literally, the finger game); it's usually played with the local sorghum-based liquor called *Kaoliang*, and the losers of each round must drain their glasses. (Westerners often describe *Kaoliang* as a cross between lighter fluid and paint thinner.)

Another popular drink is beer with a salted plum in it. Imported wines are the latest trend, fast replacing cognac as the drink of choice for cementing business relationships. Red wine holds the most appeal, partly for the luck associated with its color.

There's also a traditional belief that dark-colored alcoholic drinks exhibit *bu* (nutrition). The sophistication associated with wines has done much to crack the macho image of hard-drinking Taiwanese males.

Inhaling cigarette smoke is almost unavoidable. If you smoke, make sure you offer cigarettes to your cocelebrants; it's standard procedure in meetings, bars, offices, conference rooms and elsewhere. If you don't smoke, politely turn down the offer of a cigarette, but under no circumstances should you ask someone not to smoke around you. If you're allergic to smoke or asthmatic, you should probably decline when asked to head out for an evening of bar-hopping.

Karaoke

Just as they have a lot of faith in their drinking abilities, many Taiwanese believe they can sing. The Japanese phenomenon of *karaoke* (empty orchestra) has swept Taiwan by storm. Taiwan even has a television station devoted to this singalong pastime called KTV. Everyone is expected to participate, and even the most reticent business type can suddenly become Elvis Presley. Most of the songs are in English and the Taiwanese pride themselves on singing old standards. Try not to fall asleep during the third or fourth rendition of "You Are My Sunshine"…your turn will be next.

The Female Caveat

Businesswomen and spouses may or may not be asked to join in on evening activities. If you're the female head of a business delegation with no female Taiwanese counterpart, you may be excluded from the after-banquet festivities. Try not to be offended. It's a sign of respect, though a somewhat patronizing one. Respectable women simply don't go out drinking and smoking with the guys at night in Taiwan. In some ways, it may be a blessing, although business discussion does continue during the evening. Your best response is to make a gracious return to your hotel after instructing your next-in-command that he bears the responsibility for any business (or indignities) conducted during the evening's festivities.

Ladies of the Night

Taiwan's marital mores may be different from those in your home country. Many married men have mistresses or regularly hire prostitutes. Visiting males will be approached by and offered the services of prostitutes. (Many prostitutes work out of so-called barber shops. Hostesses, found in karaoke bars and cocktail lounges, are paid according to the amount of time they chat with a customer, who also pays for drinks.) Your hosts may even offer to pay for your pleasure. Whether you indulge or decline, no one will think the less of you.

Be aware, however, that if you're married, the incident may resurface at a later date in the form of a threat. You may also discover that the prostitute you've engaged is, in reality, an artful young man. Know also that prostitution is illegal in Taiwan and is used as a common ploy to "shake down" foreigners.

Homosexuality and lesbianism are great taboos here, though they do exist. They're considered a contradiction of the Confucian "Laws of Heaven," since no progeny can result from such unions. Indulging in, or showing an inclination toward, homosexual activity around business associates will definitely have a deleterious effect on your company's chances of success.

Gambling

Gambling is a major pastime enjoyed by both sexes. From *mah jong* parlors and *pachinko* (similar to pinball) to boat races to ping pong matches, everything is subject to a wager. Recent scandals have shown that gambling on baseball games is rigged and conducted through gangster-backed bookies, so it's best avoided.

Most of the gambling that visitors will be asked to participate in will be legal — a day at the races, for example. Keep in mind that if you've been invited by business associates, they'll be watching to see how you handle winning and, more importantly, losing.

The Arts

Taiwan is awash in visual and performing arts. Every town has Chinese opera performers and an invitation to attend is something that shouldn't be turned down. Puppet shows (*bu dai syi*), once a staple of street festivals, can still sometimes be found. And don't dishonor yourself by yawning or worse, falling asleep. It's best to read up on the art form so that you can enjoy its ancient traditions more fully.

Art galleries and religious temples are spread throughout the country. Depictions of mythological and historical events are at the core of Taiwanese culture. A walking tour through a town or city with a Taiwanese friend will give you insights into this ancient culture unavailable in books. If you can arrange an extended driving tour of the island, you'll return to your country with memories to last a lifetime.

21 Basic Mandarin Phrases

English	Chinese	Pronunciation
Yes No	Dui Bu dui	*Doo-ee* *Boo doo-ee*
Please	Qing	*Ching*
Sorry; excuse me	Dui bu qi	*Doo-ee boo chee*
Hello (on phone) Hello (in person)	Wei Ni hao	*Wei* *Knee how*
My name is _	Wo jiao _	*Wah jee-oh _*
Thank you	Xie xie	*Shee-yeh shee-yeh*
You're welcome	Bu xie	*Boo shee-yeh*
Good-bye	Zai jian	*Dzye jee-en*
I don't understand	Wo bu dong	*Wah boo dong*
How much?	Duo shao qian?	*Doo-oh shah-oh*

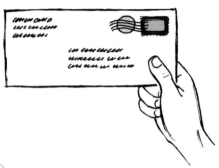

22 Correspondence

Most Taiwanese businesspeople and postal personnel can read roman characters. Because the island is relatively small, there are no postal codes and addresses are brief. For example:

Edward Lai, Vice President
Ministry of Economic Affairs
15, Foochow Street
Taipei

Correspondence being sent out of Taiwan must be placed in the red, international mailboxes. Green boxes are reserved for domestic mail. The domestic rate is about NT$5 per letter. Non-governmental package handlers, such as FedEx and UPS, are available in major cities.

Although red is generally considered an auspicious color, never use red ink for correspondence or when giving someone your address or telephone number. It's thought to convey unfriendliness.

23 Useful Numbers

Country Code: . . . .(886)
City Codes:
Taipei . . . .(02)
Kaohsiung . . . .(07)
Taichung . . . .(04)
Hsinchu . . . .(035)
Tainan . . . .(06)
Emergency Police (in Chinese) 110
Police, Taipei (in English) 311-9940
Emergency Fire (in Chinese) 119
Ambulance, Taipei (in English) 721-6316
National Central Library, Taipei 361-9132
Foreign Affairs Police (visas) 381-8341
Ministry of Economic Affairs . . . . (02) 321-2200
Ministry of Finance . . . . (02) 322-8000
International Cooperation . . . . . . (02) 391-8405
Director General of Customs . . . . (02) 741-3181
Director General of Telecom. . . . . (02) 344-3691
Council of Labor Affairs . . . . (02) 718-2512
Foreigners Service Center. . . . . . . (02) 381-8341
Government Information Office . (02) 322-8888
Taipei Central Clinic . . . . (02) 752-3315

 # Books & Internet Addresses

China in Crisis, by Sven Lindqvist. Crowell Press, New York City, New York, USA, 1965. A fascinating history of Taiwan and China.

Republic of China Yearbook, 1996. Government Information Office, ROC. A highly informative, 790-page collection of cultural and statistical information on Taiwan.

Confucius — The Analects, translated by D. C. Lau. Penguin Books, Middlesex, England, 1974. This basic text of Confucian thought provides excellent insight into the great teacher's influence on Asia.

Doing Business in Taiwan. CETRA Publications, Taipei, Taiwan, 1996.

Taiwan Business: The Portable Encyclopedia For Doing Business in Taiwan. Comprehensive 25 chapter "Country Business Guide." World Trade Press, San Rafael California, U.S.A.

Internet Addresses

Business-related website:

http://www.tptaiwan.org.tw

Anti-mainland protest information:

http://www.taiwanese.com/protest/